ADVANCE PRAISE

After the vice president's historic trip to Africa was grossly under-covered by American media, we are fortunate to have someone with deep roots to the continent and extensive relationships with and around the vice president to commit his first-hand account of the trip to the pages of history. The inadequate coverage of the vice president's historic trip to Africa often centered on where she went, who she met, or what she wore. Dr. Nii-Quartelai Quartey offers to the pages of history the important answers to "Why?"—why the first Black VP went to Africa, why it matters to the people of the African diaspora, and why the world should understand how this VP is influencing foreign policy more than any Black woman in history.

> **Terrance Woodbury**
> HIT Strategies Co-Founder
> Public Opinion Researcher

Given his own connection and relationship to the continent, Dr. Nii-Quartelai Quartey is the perfect journalist to contextualize a historic vice president's historic trip to Africa. As a Black journalist and son of Ghana, he serves as a bridge, bringing a lens to a journey that both analyzes Kamala Harris's singular political leadership on a world stage as the first Black woman to serve as the second most powerful person in the country and reflects on his personal story as a child of the diaspora and the product of two countries–grappling in real time with the meaning of his own duality and the stakes and possibilities of the moment.

Errin Haines
The 19th Editor-at-Large

Twenty-five years ago, I traveled on a US presidential delegation to Africa that changed my worldview. In his new book, *Kamala, The Motherland, and Me*, Dr. Nii-Quartelai Quartey brings me back to the memories of that trip with his own distinctive story and takes us on a new journey across continents, consciousness, time, and identity. By sharing his experiences from Nelson Mandela's visit to Oakland, California in the 1990s to Kamala Harris's trip to Accra, Ghana in 2023, Quartey builds a beautiful symbolic bridge that spans 8,000 miles of land and sea across the African diaspora. Dr. Quartey is a prominent national journalist and an intersectional community leader who unapologetically introduces his own identity as a Black gay man of Ghanaian descent to the international discourse at a moment when too many voices are being silenced and the world urgently needs to hear from credible Black thought leaders. This is a timely and important book that I hope will open eyes, minds, and hearts.

Keith Boykin
Author and Political Commentator

Kamala, The Motherland, and Me cements Dr. Nii-Quartelai Quartey's reputation as one of our community's most inspiring storytellers. Bringing forward a story of our nation's first Black

Woman vice president's trip to Tanzania, Zambia, and Ghana—his father's homeland—Quartey takes readers on a detailed journey from Air Force Two to parts of the continent of Africa that have never been visited by a sitting vice president. Painting a compelling, detailed, and often unseen side of Vice President Kamala Harris, this book belongs on every American history buff's bookshelf.

> **Richard Fowler**
> FOX News Contributor
> *Forbes* Contributing Writer

In a way that only he can, Dr. Quartey takes us on a journey of self-discovery across Africa, while covering one of the most consequential (and misunderstood) figures in American history—Vice President Kamala Harris. A fresh take that is all heart. This book is a triumph.

> **Hon. Malcolm Kenyatta**
> Pennsylvania State Representative, 181st District

Dr. Nii-Quartelai Quartey provides an up-close look not many Americans have seen of our history-making vice president, while setting the scene on a broader level of what role America should play on the world stage. It also serves as a vivid introduction to Dr. Quartey's unique expertise, which I'm excited to have introduced nationwide through this important read for aspiring journalists and public servants alike.

> **Hon. Karen Bass**
> Mayor of Los Angeles
> Former Chair of Subcommittee on Africa, Global Health, and Global Human Rights
> US House of Representatives Foreign Affairs Committee Member

Dr. Nii-Quartelai Quartey approaches all his work with a fervor for the topic, a respect for the reader, and a historical mindset of the person he's covering. This book is no different. Kamala Harris's trip to Africa served as a turning point in her vice presidency, and there's no one better suited to tell that story than Dr. Quartey.

Eugene Daniels
Politico White House Reporter
Politico Playbook Co-Author
White House Correspondents' Association President

I loved the way in which Dr. Nii-Quartelai unfolded this narrative that Black America has been waiting for! This behind-the-scenes look connects insider information/experiences to the external agendas facing our nation's first Black vice president and changed the way that I see the White House. Black leadership matters, and this book helped me to understand that the intentional attacks faced by Kamala Harris are the common challenges faced by so many of us coming from communities of color, fighting to make a difference in public service, while remaining committed to cultural competence.

Paul Henderson
Veteran Prosecutor
San Francisco Department of Police Accountability
Executive Director

More than adequately told, Dr. Nii-Quartelai Quartey shares the untold story of a history-making United States vice president. Instructive, informative, insightful—a necessary read to better understand Kamala Harris.

Tavis Smiley
Host of *The Tavis Smiley Show*

KAMALA

THE MOTHERLAND
AND ME

KAMALA

THE MOTHERLAND AND ME

An Invitation to Challenge Your Assumptions
about Madam Vice President,
Africa, and Ourselves

DR. NII-QUARTELAI QUARTEY

Press 49
4980 South Alma School Road
Suite 2-493
Chandler, Arizona 85248

Published by Press 49, a division of BMH Companies, Chandler, Arizona.

Volume pricing is available to bulk orders placed by corporations, associations, and others. For bulk order details and for media inquiries, please contact Press 49 at info@press49.com or 833.PRESS49 (833.773.7749).

FIRST EDITION

Library of Congress Control Number: 2024907907

ISBN: 978-1-953315-42-7 (paperback)
ISBN: 978-1-953315-43-4 (eBook)

POL046000 POLITICAL SCIENCE/Commentary & Opinion
HIS037000 HISTORY/World
BIO026000 BIOGRAPHY & AUTOBIOGRAPHY/Memoirs

Cover design by Artichoked Creative
Interior design by Medlar Publishing Solutions Pvt Ltd., India
Printed in the United States of America
Back cover photo by Corey Fletcher

CONTENTS

AUTHOR'S NOTE

This book is a reflection of a dream journalism assignment. It is a re-examination of our historic US vice president, Kamala Harris. It is a review of the promise and pitfalls on the continent of Africa. And it is a sometimes-difficult conversation with ourselves. It is not intended to be flattering or unflattering. But I do intend to take you on a journey that stirred up experiences, ideas, hopes, and fears with some radical imagination. With personal transparency, I provide a unique lens of examination into widely held assumptions about Vice President Harris, the continent of Africa, being a Black American gay man raised by parents who grew up an ocean apart, and the intersectionality of it all.

Throughout the book, you will see that I refer to Vice President Harris in different ways. When I use the title of vice president, I am talking about her in her official capacity as one of our heads of state. I am talking about her as somebody who is second in line to the presidency and one of the highest-ranking elected officials in the United States.

My intention is to offer her and the office the highest level of respect, even when I engage in critique.

When I refer to her as Kamala, when I say, "We are Kamala and Kamala is us," I am referring to her as kinfolk and not just skin folk. When I codeswitch and I refer to her as Kamala, no disrespect is meant by it. I do it as a device to engender cultural connection and to eliminate any barriers to that connection.

I also use the term "we" often in this book, and I do so in reference to the Black community through a wide lens, inclusive of all the different flavors and demonstrations of Black identity. It is intended to serve as an invitation to anyone and everyone of African descent as well as those who are in community with people of African descent.

I challenge you to walk away from this book with a fresh perspective on the opportunities that exist between America and African nations. I challenge you to walk away with a careful examination of your assumptions about Vice President Kamala Harris. Lastly, I challenge you to carefully consider the interconnectedness of Black people across the African diaspora.

ACKNOWLEDGEMENTS

All praises to the Most High for choosing me to be a vessel for this story of enormous personal and professional significance in the modern age of growing misinformation and disinformation, perpetuated by bad actors both foreign and domestic. Over the course of the past year, while I've been working on this assignment, some friends and peers alike have been surprised to learn that Vice President Kamala Harris's historic trip to Africa even happened. Their lack of awareness is perhaps a function of many things, including the noisy media environment; limited attention spans; an insatiable social media appetite for snackable content; and often narrow media coverage of Vice President Harris with a hyperfocus on her flaws, likeability, and relatability at the expense of examining her as a possibility model.

Many thanks to my mom, Debra Quartey, and my dad, the late Joseph K. Quartey, for raising me to be courageous, to see real possibilities in others and the world. David, Speedy, Quaye, and Paajoe–being your youngest brother has been one of my greatest teachers in life, even when I didn't understand the assignment. Through you and each of my nieces and nephews, I continue to learn even more about the potency of human connection. This season of my life and assignment have meant less time in your company, but I pray the sacrifice leaves you feeling proud, not ignored.

Many thanks to my husband, Montré Burton, for being a demonstration of what's possible in life and love. Nobody knows what it takes for us to show up as light in the world better than you. Thanks for keeping me lifted throughout this marathon adventure. Aunt Lahoma, Aunt Darlene, Ms. Emma, Mrs. White, Angie Burton Morgan, and my Norfolk Family—thank you for believing in me, rooting for my rise through each of life's inevitable plot twists.

To Tavis Smiley, your legacy and enduring wisdom continue to be a source of real possibilities for me. To Emil Wilbekin, Native Son, and Bayard Baldwin, thank you for being a bright light in my world. To Stephen Brown, James DuBose, Cortney Hicks-Lanier, and the FOX Television/FOX SOUL team that ultimately allowed me the opportunity to pursue this assignment, thank you. To Erika Winston, my devoted editor, thank you for giving me your very best so that I might offer the world my very best. To my personal council of advisors, thank you for your continued support, encouragement, mentorship, fellowship, love, subtle and grand inspiration. You know who you are, and you know what you mean to me. You all liberate different parts of me, and I love you for it.

Many thanks to Madam Vice President Kamala Harris and the entire White House team that worked over a year to plan a historic Africa trip, unburdened by the past and motivated by what could be. Your reflections, one year later in a time such as this, were as illuminating as they were thought-provoking. To every person who participated in on- and off-the-record interviews, this book wouldn't be the same without your generosity of time, insights, and wisdom. To my fellow White House Correspondents' Association members on the trip and local press on the Continent, thank you for welcoming me on this journey with open arms, your continued collegiality, and budding friendship.

Finally, it's not lost on me that the ancestors have conspired with my editors, book cover illustrator, and publisher to take you on an unforgettable journey of consequence. Many thanks to each of you for trusting me enough to take this journey. Weekdays on my KBLA Talk 1580 radio show and podcast, *A More Perfect Union*, I end every show spreading the wisdom of the late NAACP National Board Member Willis Edwards by saying "Don't panic, organize. Do what you can, from where you are, with what you have." In some grand and subtle ways, this trip may have done exactly this. You be the judge.

CHAPTER ONE

A CELEBRATED WELCOME

"By 2050, one in four people in the entire world will be on this very continent. One in four. That, of course, means what happens on this continent impacts the entire world."[1] These were some of the first words spoken by Vice President Kamala Harris as she addressed the people of Ghana at Black Star Square. Constructed in the early 1960s, the Square commemorates Ghana's independence from British colonial rule. It features a distinctive black star monument at its center, symbolizing the country's struggle for its freedom. Listening to the vice president at the start of this dream assignment felt like a call to action that would frame this momentous trip from beginning to end—a trip that would test her abilities on a world stage and challenge the underlying assumptions associated with the US vice president, the continent of Africa, and the Black American experience of the past versus the future. But it was also a trip that would strengthen my personal connection to the homeland of my father and the continent of my mother's ancestors.

When I attended the NAACP Image Awards in February of 2023, I had no idea that one simple conversation would lead to the biggest assignment I'd had since returning to journalism. For almost fifteen years, I worked inside and outside of government on advocacy and public affairs. Like so many of us, the pandemic pushed me to ask some difficult questions about my life. I wasn't feeling fulfilled or challenged to do my best work, so I decided to take a leap of faith and return to my first love of journalism. Making this pivot worked out well for me from the beginning. The day after I resigned, I appeared on MSNBC's *The Sunday Show* with Jonathan Capehart. Soon after that, I began contributing to TheGrio and never looked back. Since then, I have hosted a daily radio broadcast called *A More Perfect Union*, and I previously co-anchored FOX SOUL's *Black Report*, a daily news show produced for FOX Television and FOX SOUL streaming platform. That is how I landed myself a seat at the Image Awards where a friend who worked for the Biden-Harris administration casually mentioned that the vice president was preparing to go to Africa. With immediate interest, I asked if they knew where in Africa she would visit. They told me that Ghana was on the list, along with some other countries they were unsure about. I knew instinctively that I had to go on this trip. I didn't know how it was going to happen, but I knew I had to go.

I could barely wait until Monday morning to reach out to a contact of mine at the White House. She connected me with the VP's team, and I emailed them a concise pitch to join the press corps covering the trip. I shared my ancestry as a first-generation Ghanaian-American and explained my intention to tell the story of this trip to the viewers of the *Black Report*, my daily radio show listeners at KBLA Talk 1580, my podcast listeners, and the audiences that I reach through my cable news appearances. My pitch must have resonated with the VP's team because it did not take them long to respond.

"You're invited!" were the first words I saw as I opened the message with much anticipation and a long list of questions running through my head. Would I be traveling on the plane with the press corps, or would I be pre-credentialed to meet on location once they got there? Would I be allowed on the Ghana leg only, or would it be all three of the scheduled countries? For a host of different reasons, reporters sometimes don't travel along with the principal government official on the plane, but they will instead meet them at the destination. I wondered if I would have to do the same. After reading through the long list of required shots, I learned that they hadn't committed to me being on the plane. They basically told me "Here's the itinerary and the list of countries. You'll be credentialed, but you have to get there on your own." Of course, it wasn't the ideal circumstance, but it was not enough to keep me from this amazing trip. I had some decisions to make. Things could get really expensive really quickly, so I had to decide whether or not I was going to do just the Ghana leg or visit all three countries.

At almost the last minute, the VP's team informed me that a seat had opened up on Air Force Two, and I could be on the plane for all three legs. I obviously took the seat, but there were still some challenges to overcome. Typically, when members of the press travel with government officials, the travel related expenses are covered by their associated media outlet. For me, that meant approaching the executives at FOX Television and FOX SOUL about funding my trip. I excitedly told my team about this dream opportunity I had to travel to the continent of Africa with the first Black woman vice president of the United States. A front row seat to Black history—American history—in real time. The lack of enthusiasm among some key team members was palpable. Discussions around integrating the trip into the show were not pursued, and one key team member even told me that the trip was not newsworthy. The network did not see the return on investment that I saw. Though they were not willing to pay my travel expenses, I was willing to pay the entire cost of the trip out of my own pocket because I believed it was that important for history's sake.

On March 25, 2023, days before Vice President Harris gave her historic Black Star Square speech, I set out on the assignment of a lifetime. As we boarded Air Force Two, I was surprised to see so many Black people involved with the operations of this auspicious airplane. From the very start, it felt as though a substantial number of people who had their hands on this trip had a connection to the continent. And if they did not have a direct connection, they had a respect, at the very least, and in some cases, a reverence for it. The departure date fell on the International Day of Remembrance of the Victims of Slavery and the Transatlantic Slave

Trade, and I knew that could not be a coincidence. Even the departure date was purposeful, and there was a sense in the air that we were embarking on history in the making.

Landing in Accra was a truly special moment. As the plane taxied, my ears filled with melodic sounds of drums beating from the runway. Combined with the cheers of the crowd, the sound was so powerful that I could hear it even over the roar of the plane engine. The relationship between the drumbeat and the heartbeat is inseparable. For me, that heartbeat started in the San Francisco Bay Area, much like the vice president. But an ocean away, my heartbeat was still in sync with the drumbeat I heard upon our arrival. It felt like that sense of connection you get when you meet someone for the first time, and you are so aligned that you feel like you have known them for a lifetime.

While this was not my first time on the continent, nor my first time in Ghana, it was my first time experiencing it in this way. I felt an awesome connection between my heartbeat and the drumbeat.

While I could see reactions of appreciation from some of the other Black reporters on the plane, as a Ghanaian-American, our arrival hit differently for me. Yes, I was on the plane with my people, but the crowds that gathered outside were also my people. My worlds collided in the most beautiful of ways. I was there as a professional journalist, but my connection to the moment was also deeply personal. As I gathered my belongings in preparation to leave the plane, I intentionally took a moment to take it all in.

WE'RE ALL IN

The overarching theme of the vice president's remarks was reinforcing the commitment of the Biden-Harris Administration to building partnerships with African nations. "As President Joe Biden said, at the U.S.-Africa Leaders Summit last December, we're all in on Africa," she said.[2] "We are all in because African nations play such a critical role on issues of global importance, issues that matter to the American people and to the world. Issues like food security, the climate crisis, public health, and resilient supply chains.

"We are all in because African leadership is critical to global peace and security, and African nations are essential partners at the United Nations and in support of international rules and norms. We are all in because the fates of the American people and of America and the continent of Africa are interconnected and interdependent.

"We are all in because there are longstanding ties between our people. We have an intertwined history, some of which is painful and some of which is prideful, and all of which we must acknowledge, teach, and never forget. Because of this history, this continent, of course, has a special significance for me personally as the first Black vice president of the United States of America."

Vice President Harris went on to explain that being all in "... means that the United States is committed to strengthen our partnerships across the continent of Africa–partnerships with governments, the private sector, civil society, and all of you. Partnerships based on openness, inclusiveness, candor, shared interests, and mutual benefits.

"And to be clear, America will be guided not by what we can do for our African partners, but what we can do with our African partners. Together, we will address the challenges we face and the incredible opportunities ahead."

NII-QUARTELAI QUARTEY

In February 1990, Nelson Mandela walked away from South Africa's Victor Verster Prison near Cape Town as a free man after twenty-seven years in captivity. That summer, he traveled to the US for an eight-city tour, and the Oakland Coliseum was his final stop. More than 58,000 people packed the stadium to hear the iconic leader speak, and my family was among them. I was six years old, and I remember my parents piling me and my brothers into our midnight blue Jeep Cherokee. Along with my godparents and their families, we all drove from Concord, California to Oakland where we heard Mandela speak.

That experience had an incredible impact on me. At six years old, I did not have a fully developed awareness of Mandela and his story. But my young mind was very clear that this was someone who could have chosen to be bitter but instead chose optimism. He chose to channel that optimism in ways that brought people together, people that may not share the same race or gender or background. He used his power for good, and I knew that, no matter what I did in my life, I wanted to be an extension of that. I wanted to use whatever gifts I had to help people see themselves in one another. To help bring people together and facilitate understanding, compassion, and empathy. To be a bridge between some of the great divisions in the world.

My parents gave me a name that reflects my sense of responsibility for others. In case you haven't noticed, I have a very uncommon name, and the intention behind it is "caregiver of the family." It's a very Ghanaian name, and it's a lot of name with nineteen letters in my whole name and every vowel but "o." I was in college before I learned that native Ghanaians spell and pronounce my first name differently. In fact, I have what's considered the anglicized version of my name. So, when I'm around fellow Ghanaians and I introduce myself, I often receive a polite side eye that says "I think I know what he's saying, but how does he not know his name?" For years, when I had to introduce myself to members of the Ghanaian side of my family for the first time, I was really self-conscious about it. At times, I even tried to avoid it or hurry through the pronunciation because I didn't want to confront the quandary around my name. Sometimes, I'd get scolded for saying my own name "incorrectly," which caused a bit of embarrassment. Your name is something sacred. Your parents gave it to you at birth. And in Ghanaian culture, naming ceremonies are particularly important because your name indicates what tribe you're a part of. No matter where you are in the world, you can always come home based on your name. If you show up at the airport in Accra and give them your name, they know exactly where your ancestral home is. So, to flub your name, at least in the eyes of other Ghanaians, is not good. It is not good at all.

My name alone created a demand for cultural fluency. When I'm with my African American side of my family or with my friends, they know I have a very African name. Just starting with my name alone, the sense of belonging is different. I belong in that centerpiece of the Venn diagram where two sides overlap. The Ghanaians know I must be American born. And the African Americans know that I am truly African American. You are seen differently—literally move differently—because of that. I am very intentional about my name and how people pronounce it. I've had to deal with this my whole life, and it's really important to me that folks understand that you should never take liberties with people's names. As I've gotten older and wiser, I've become less tolerant of people taking liberties with my name. I've had very smart, accomplished, well-traveled people with a heightened cultural fluency ask me if I had a nickname. And my answer is always "no." I don't do it in a nasty sort of way, but I do say it with all ten toes down. If people are unwilling to call you by your name, then they're probably unwilling to fully recognize your humanity. And my humanity is not up for negotiation.

Just as I'm particular about folks' names, I'm also very sympathetic to people's pronouns. I still have my challenges, but I always attempt to do my best to call others as they wish to be called. I'm not going to willfully call folks by the wrong pronouns, but for added measure I might call them by their names in order to avoid misgendering them. If somebody wants you to call them by a specific pronoun, it shouldn't be any sweat off your back to do your best to get it right. I do recognize that, in conversation, you may have to retrain your brain. I have certainly errored many times on "they/them" pronouns. I may have to consciously think about it, but I make the effort because their humanity is also not up for negotiation.

I give a lot of credit to my parents for raising me to be a global citizen. My mom grew up near the height of the civil rights movement in Florida before moving to Texas where she went to college and met my dad who was born into colonial Ghana and was seven years old when Ghana declared its independence from the British. I am the product of the collision of those experiences in a place like California and, more specifically, a place like the San Franisco Bay Area. The Bay Area is a multicultural bastion of the country. When you look at the history of the gay rights movement, the Black power movement, the women's liberation movement, and the anti-war movement, a lot of them have very formative building experiences in the Bay Area. It's a very special place in general. And I couldn't imagine becoming all of who I am without having been exposed to that history. So, it's no surprise to me that it also produced Vice President Harris, a leader who positions herself as a citizen of the world.

I grew up in a house of five boys (my oldest brother David and I have a fifteen-year age difference), an extroverted father, my somewhat introverted mom, and an insatiable curiosity. I was raised to give a damn and to understand that to whom much is given, much is required. My parents instilled a tremendous sense of duty in me. I've taken that to mean being in service to the human family, being in service to humanity, and bringing that to my work. I had the kind of dad who would call me in the house from playing outside and sit me down on the couch to watch something important on C-SPAN. I had the kind of dad who would take me to public lectures at UC Berkeley. I had the kind of dad who challenged my thinking and encouraged me to be a critical thinker and encouraged me to consider different points of view—some of which may not be my own. My dad was an environmental chemist, but I think he really wanted to be a lawyer. He even took some law classes at UC Hastings, which is now known as University of California College of Law, to feed his curiosity. He had a curiosity about people and about the world, and it passed on to me. I feel fortunate that, in this act of my life, I get to pursue that curiosity in ways that he would've never imagined. He would have been infuriated by the book bans and erasure of Black history that is happening across the country as a violation of his constitution and the American constitution.

When I think about my mom's side of the family, there's at least an oral history of enslaved people. It amazes me to think that my bloodline goes that far back to a time when that side of my family was considered three-fifths of a person. Knowing the history on both sides of my family helps me to be really clear-eyed about my work today. I have a daily show on a Black radio station in Los Angeles and a podcast that can be unapologetically Black; unapologetically progressive; and dare I say, unapologetically pro-democracy. I'm sure there are a lot of other things I could be doing with my time that might be even more lucrative, but I see my work as greatly important in the public discourse at this moment. Similarly, this book will also be very important in the public discourse as an act of resilience in this current era of book bans. I felt called to write a book that pushed back against this assault on one of the pillars of any great democracy—the freedom of the press and the freedom of expression.

KAMALA HARRIS

More than 8,000 people, mostly young in age, awaited Vice President Harris as she arrived at Black Star Square to deliver her remarks. I was not surprised to see the crowd that awaited her, but this felt different—more special and energetic. Watching the crowd's reaction to the vice president, I was struck by the stark difference between the incredibly warm reception she received and the narrative around her that has inundated the mainstream American media since she first entered the race as a presidential candidate in 2019. The unwarranted level of blatant and indirect criticism has been highly problematic in and of itself, but its influence on the opinions of voters, particularly Black voters, is even more troublesome as we inch closer to an incredibly consequential presidential election of 2024.

Vice President Harris has a favorability problem that extends across gender, age, and race. As of January 2024, 42 percent of US adults surveyed expressed a very unfavorable opinion of her, while 39 percent had either a very favorable or somewhat favorable opinion, according to Statista.[3] Compared to past vice presidents, at the same point in their respective tenures, her net favorability is slightly lower than that of former vice president Mike Pence. But it is far lower than the ratings of Joe Biden, Dick Cheney, and Al Gore during their vice presidencies.[4] There are many variables surrounding these numbers, including some legitimate critiques, but this first Black, Indian, female vice president of the United States is also dealing with a convergence of biases and prejudices that no other US vice president has ever contended with before. From the characterization of her remarks as "word salads" to the subtle and not so subtle questioning of her leadership abilities, Vice President Harris is a case study in misogynoir.

Rashad Robinson, the president of racial justice organization Color of Change, spoke to me about this in my interview with him. "When she was chosen to be on the ticket," he said, "I knew that there would be a deep level of racist and misogynist attacks against her that would not only impact how she was viewed but would also impact the ways in which Black women leadership and Black women in power were viewed. And so, we were very clear about the civil rights commitment we had to have around being very clear that we treat the vice president like a politician.

That doesn't mean being sycophants. We are going to hold her accountable and push her. But we're also not going to pretend like the playing field is equal."[5]

He said that we should be able to disagree with politicians that we respect and admire. "I have disagreements with Kamala Harris, and I have disagreements with policy positions. There are things I may have critique on, and we can hold those multiple things together. I am not one to pretend that those things don't exist just because she is a Black woman, and I am also not going to be tricked and fooled into the idea that she also will not be on the receiving end of certain types of bad faith attacks that are not about her or her job or her worth."[6]

Having been present in Ghana for the vice president's Black Star Square speech, Robinson shared his response to seeing the reception extended to her by the people of Ghana. "That moment of her showing up in a foreign country and having those many people cheering for her was a moment that spoke to a type of world leadership that we oftentimes don't give her credit for. Later that night, while watching Ghanaian news, I saw all of these interviews of young women talking about what she meant to them in terms of being a young woman who chose her own career path."[7] He pointed out the fact that many young women on the continent of Africa are expected to move into having and raising families well before they have opportunities to make decisions about a career path. "Yet, the women speaking [in these interviews] were young journalists and young lawyers. Some of them were in medical school, and they were all talking about what the vice president's choices and leadership meant to them."[8]

Assumptions about Vice President Harris don't stop with racism and sexism. Among Black voters, her ratings largely mirror those of President Biden, but a generational gap shows young Black voters as least favorable towards her.[9] Vice President Harris's positivity rating for voters over fifty years old is often twenty or more points higher than that of younger Black voters. These differences are largely based in people's opinions about the vice president's professional past and her connection with the criminal justice system. She is seen as the woman who put Black men into the prison system, and her proximity to Blackness is consistently questioned. Yes, she went to Howard University, and yes, she is a member of Alpha Kappa Alpha Sorority, Inc. (AKA); but that does not resonate with everyone. A lot of the pomp and circumstance around her vice presidency came from a particular community of Black college graduates, Black members of the Divine Nine, and Black folks from particular communities. But there are some Black folks who will view the pride that she has as a Bison and the pride she has as an AKA with being a bourgeois Black person. Right from the start, there are a few aspects of her professional, personal, and political biography that may be at odds with different segments of Black folks. As somebody who's earned a number of academic credentials, I get how some other people look at her and the narrative around her and jump to conclusions, but I hope that this book will challenge some of those assumptions.

In my life before journalism, I worked on a number of advocacy campaigns, doing policy advocacy work in coalitions with a wide range of people. I saw a distinct difference between when folks were on the outside of power and then when they were in the seat of power. Being a decision-maker requires a different set of tactics, a different kind of talk. And I think sometimes our coalitions don't always appreciate folks that may have been on the periphery that are now in the center; they're now in the seat tower. There's not enough appreciation of the transition time in terms of finding their voice, finding their sea legs. I don't think that we extend enough grace. And I think that's a struggle that Black people don't have a monopoly on. It's a struggle that queer people don't have a monopoly on. It's certainly not a struggle that women have a monopoly on.

THE CONTINENT OF AFRICA

Eugene Daniels, White House Correspondent for Politico and president of the White House Correspondents' Association, was a member of the press corps that accompanied the vice president to Ghana. In my interview with Daniels, he shared that the Black Star Square speech stood out in his mind as the thesis statement for why she made the trip. "She talked about innovation and the United States being all in on the continent of Africa. She talked about working with Africans and not just giving them things, and that is something that you heard as a criticism about the relationship between the United States and the continent of Africa for decades, that American leaders often treat the continent as a charity case, a place to give money, to give aid and leave. But what we heard from leaders and people who live there was, 'No, we make stuff here. We don't need your charity. We might need some investment, like every country needs some investment, to jumpstart these programs, but we don't need your charity.' Vice President Harris obviously got that."[10]

Daniels also talked about the response of the people who braved the extreme heat to be in attendance. "People get excited when American leaders come to their country, but to see a Black woman who looked like them, someone whose family had possibly come through Cape Coast and come from that continent, it was deeply meaningful for them. But it also puts pressure on the vice president because they are holding her up to a standard of, 'Hey, you look just like us. We have a seat at the table.' So, now, Ghanaians are going to be looking at the United States to prove that they want to be a partner, and Vice President Harris is a perfect example of that promise being made by the administration."[11]

The aspects of the speech that resonated with Daniels also resonated with me. This could have been a classic public health trip, the type of humanitarian trip that we usually see on the continent. But the vice president decided to focus on entrepreneurship instead of the usual narrative around famine and disease. She was determined to show folks the possibilities that exist today across the diaspora, the opportunities for ripe new investment.

"Innovation, I believe to be the pursuit of what can be unburdened by what has been," she stated in her remarks. "Innovation results in one's ability not only to see, but to do things differently. New methods, new products, new approaches, new ideas. We innovate to be more effective and to solve problems. From the invention of new technology to the origin of social movements, innovation has come about by challenging the premise, questioning the status quo, and bold thinking. And so, to the young leaders here today, you, by your very nature, are dreamers and innovators.

"And so, to you I say: It is your spark, your creativity, and your determination that will drive the future. And with that then, African ideas and innovations will shape the future of the world. And so, we must invest in African ingenuity and creativity, which will unlock incredible economic growth and opportunities, not only for the people of the 54 countries that make up this diverse continent, but for the American people and people around the world. So, the Biden-Harris administration and the American people stand ready to partner with you, to help accelerate the innovation and entrepreneurship that is already underway."[12]

The power of the vice president's words grew in importance and relevance for me as the trip progressed. I recognized that a lot of what the people of Africa are wanting is not radically different from what Black folks here in the United States want and are open to. We want access to capital, too. We want people to invest in our creative economy, too. We want to be able to tap into the power of artificial intelligence technologies to make our lives better, to make our businesses run more efficiently, without trampling on our basic civil and human rights. When the vice president talked about digital inclusion, we understood what that meant. That was one of my biggest takeaways from traveling on all three legs of the trip. A lot of what she was talking about, a lot of what she was promoting wasn't radically different from what she's been talking about and promoting here in the United States. So, this idea that what Black Americans want and what Ghanaians or Tanzanians or Zambians or Africans at large want is somehow different, it just is not true.

Forgive my ignorance, but I was surprised to see journalists in Ghana and Zambia very concerned about climate change. Of the very few questions that the press corps was allowed to ask them during these press conferences, those are the questions they chose. I was taken aback. I thought to myself, "Wow, I don't think a lot of Black folks in the United States would think that Africans care so much about climate change." In the US, we often hear the topic referred to as some type of San Francisco liberal issue, but that is not true. Climate change is a prevalent issue across the continent of Africa, and there are talented individuals there who are working to minimize the damage.

The vice president's trip and the purposeful message she attached to it showcased the opportunity that the United States has to invest more in entrepreneurship to spur the creative economy, for example, to bridge the gap between men and women who have access to the internet across the continent. Look at what we can learn in terms of climate resilience by partnering more with AgriTech leaders in the AgriTech industry across the continent. Look at the important conversations we should be having around strengthening democracy and resisting the temptation for authoritarian rule. Folks may not give her credit, but on her watch and on the president's watch, we're seeing Africa emerge as more of a player when it comes to US foreign policy.

Vice President Harris's Arrival to Ghana, March 2023

Vice President Harris Day 1 Newspaper Headlines in Ghana

Vice President Harris Newspaper Headlines in Ghana

Vice President Harris's Speech at Black Star Square, Ghana

Aerial View of Black Star Square Speech, Ghana

Advance Team Lead Dorien Paul Blythers and Nii-Quartelai Snap a Photo Arrival in Ghana, March 2023

Nii-Quartelai's Arrival to Ghana, March 2023

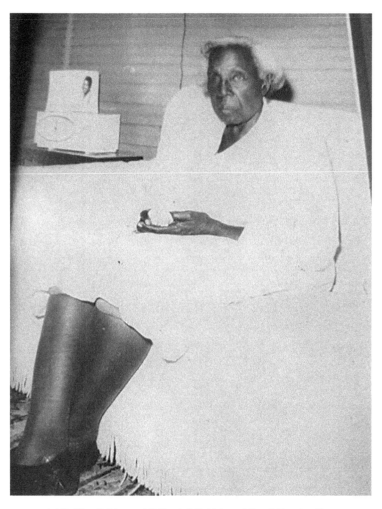

Addie Mae Robinson, Nii-Quartelai's Maternal Great Grandmother

Willie Robinson, Nii-Quartelai's Maternal Great Grandfather

Addie Mae Thomas, Nii-Quartelai's Maternal Grandmother

Dave Thomas, Nii-Quartelai's Maternal Grandfather

Joseph Quartey and Helena Baidoo, Nii-Quartelai's Dad and Paternal Grandmother

Nii-Quartelai's Parents, Debra and Joseph Quartey, on Their Wedding Day

US Army Staff Sergeant David Lee Thomas, Nii-Quartelai's Uncle

Nii-Quartelai and Brothers David, James, John, and Joseph Quartey Jr

Young Nii-Quartelai at 8 Years Old at Older Brother's De La Salle High School
Graduation, Concord, CA, 1992

Nii-Quartelai at High School Graduation with Maternal and Paternal Grandmothers

Nii-Quartelai Visiting Quartey Memorial Secondary School, October 2011

Nii-Quartelai and His Brother David at Quartey Memorial Secondary School, October 2011

Quartey Memorial Crest on Composition Book, October 2011

Nii-Quartelai and Montre Burton's Wedding, July 2015

CHAPTER TWO

BREAKING BREAD

In March of 1957, Martin Luther King Jr. and Coretta Scott King accepted an invitation from the Prime Minister of Ghana to attend the celebration of the country's independence from European colonization. Their presence symbolized alliance and a recognition of the parallels that existed between the people of Africa and the struggle for civil rights in the United States. In March of 2023, Ghana's President Nana Akufo-Addo and First Lady Rebecca Akufo-Addo extended an invitation to leaders like Vice President Harris, NAACP president and CEO Derrick Johnson, artist Kehinde Wiley, film director Spike Lee, and Howard University president Dr. Wayne A. I. Frederick to join them in Accra for an official state dinner. As I stood with the press corps and listened to the vice president speak about their intertwined histories, I felt a strong connection and profound sense of gratitude for the radical imagination of the barrier breaking Black Americans who visited Ghana decades earlier—a connection that I had never before explored.

Connecting History

In 1874, the British formally colonized the area we now know as Ghana, and in 1925, they formally stifled the voices of Ghanaians with the creation of a provincial councils of paramount chiefs.[1] While some tribal interests were included in the formal declaration, they remained a far second to those of the British. Any voice given to Ghanaians was limited, which drove a wedge between chiefs and their more educated subjects. The desire for greater independence grew louder throughout the 1930s and 1940s before coming to a head in 1948 when widespread protests broke out in Accra and other major Ghanaian cities where European businesses were looted and destroyed. In the aftermath, members of the United Gold Coast Convention (UGCC) party were held responsible and arrested, elevating them to the level of heroes in the eyes of the Ghanaian people. Kwame Nkrumah, one of the arrestees, broke away from the UGCC to form the Convention People's Party and push for independence. He was ultimately elected to the position of prime minister, and in 1956, the new assembly authorized the request for independence from the British Commonwealth.

On March 6, 1957, Ghana officially declared its independence from the colonial rule of Britain. Leaders held a grand ceremony at Accra's Independence Square where thousands of Ghanaians gathered to hear the West African country's first president declare, "Ghana, your beloved country is free forever."[2] Along with the African dignitaries in attendance, there were also numerous Black American leaders taking part in the celebration, including Dr. Martin Luther King Jr. and his wife Coretta, who were personally invited by Prime Minister Nkrumah.[3] At midnight, Dr. King joined a crowd on the Accra polo grounds to witness the national flag of Britain be replaced by the flag of Ghana.

Ghana's movement to independence started a wave of independence movements across the continent of Africa, but it also greatly influenced the fight for equality taking place in the United States. Black people across the African diaspora recognized their shared histories of racial oppression and struggles against colonialism. This historical connection ignited a spirit of racial solidarity with Ghana's independence as a beacon of hope. In America, Black folks took inspiration from Ghana's liberation. They took on the principles of the Pan-African movement, recognizing the profound connection, intertwining history, and shared ideologies. Pan-Africanism is based on the premise that people of African descent have common interests and should be unified regardless of where they live in the world. W. E. B. Du Bois was pivotal to the shaping of modern Pan-Africanism, organizing the first Pan-African Conference in 1900.[4]

NAACP national president Derrick Johnson talked with me about the role the NAACP played during this transformational time in Black history, explaining that the organization took part in the advisory group to help establish and advise the formation of the African National Congress (ANC) in 1912. "Many African leaders who rose up in the late forties, fifties, and sixties were educated at historically Black colleges and universities (HBCUs) in the United States," he said. "One of [the NAACP] founders, W. E. B. Du Bois, is laid to rest in Accra, and he was one of the foremost thought leaders in terms of Pan-Africanism. Tanzanian leader Julius Nyerere created a safe haven for many individuals involved in the global struggle for human dignity of African people, whether it was the training camps in Morogoro that the ANC retreated to—and actually Nelson Mandela's brother, who was a fighter for the ANC, is laid to rest in Morogoro—or a village called Black Panther Village. Many African Americans that had to flee the country, such as Black Panther activists as a result of COINTELPRO, found safe havens in Tanzania."[5]

Speaking with Johnson opened my eyes to the breadth of love and safety that existed between African countries and American civil rights leaders. He explained that when movement leaders realized that they were targets and had to leave the country, those moves were, at times, facilitated through some of our brightest stars. "Fundraising by Harry Belafonte helped Stokely Carmichael to leave. And you had individuals like Maya Angelou who also went to Ghana. Bob Moses and Courtland Cox, who were Student Nonviolent Coordinating Committee activists, set up camp in Tanzania. Dorie Ladner and Joyce Ladner were in Egypt with Haile Selassie before the government failed there. And ironically, Willie Ricks, who was a Student Nonviolent Coordinating Committee activist, was in Uganda before Idi Amin created some of what took place."[6]

Johnson told me that these connections of the African diaspora are nothing new with a long history of mutual interest in protecting our bodies and our property from exploitation for others' wealth, which extends to the Caribbean.

"When Aristide was toppled in Haiti, one of the places he came was to the NAACP national convention. Randall Robinson helped support those efforts, which he also did for Nelson Mandela. Mandela planned to make three trips [during the year after his release] to be with Yasser Arafat, Palestine Liberation Organization, who supported the ANC for many years, to be with Castro who supported the ANC and liberation struggles for many years, and to the United States to meet with African American leaders because that was the genesis of the support to overturn apartheid. And so, there's well-established decades, if not century-long, cross-communications throughout the African diaspora."[7]

This point in the conversation came full circle for me as I thought about my six-year-old self standing amongst the crowd with my neck stretched high watching Nelson Mandela speak at the Oakland Coliseum. Johnson was confirming so much of the connection that I felt to Mandela's words and presence, even though I couldn't explain it at the time. I was in awe of his capacity to transcend his pain and sacrifice to become a beacon of hope for his people and the world. My young mind couldn't appreciate the fullness of Mandela's long walk to freedom quite yet, but that day left me with a visual of what it can look and feel like to overcome. Now, in the process of telling this story to Johnson, I was learning the historical thread that ran through the indelible impression that moment left in me.

Johnson recalled that when Mandela attended the NAACP national convention, people walked the streets outside, protesting his embrace of Yasser Arafat and Fidel Castro. "He was very clear in his response, saying 'You make the mistake of thinking that your enemy is my enemy. In truth, these are individuals who supported me, so I am giving thanks to them for their support.'" Johnson, who attended the convention as a college-aged student, said, "It was eye-opening to understand that our movements are not local and parochial. It is actually global, and it is based on a common thread of not being exploited as a readily available source of cheap labor or not being exploited for the wealth that we actually sit on, whether it's in countries where we are the majority population or in municipalities where we have governing control."[8]

JOLLOF RICE

The aesthetic of the Ghanaian state dinner was very impressive with dimly lit lighting and soft music. There were beautiful flowers and rows of rectangular tables where guests were seated. It gave me the sense that the Ghanaian president was rolling out the red carpet. It felt special and very Zamunda-like for all the *Coming to America* fans.

Vice President Harris thanked President Akufo-Addo for his invitation to her, along with the welcome he had extended to Black Americans in previous years. "We are joined today by incredible leaders from Ghana and throughout the continent," she said.[9] "And here with us tonight are also individuals from the United States who represent the glorious beauty of the African diaspora. We have with us on this trip Oscar and Emmy winners, CEOs and media publishers, civil rights leaders and advocates, artists and academics, dignitaries and diplomats.

"And, Mr. President, you are personally responsible for welcoming and encouraging the connection of the diaspora to this continent. Because of you, Mr. President, hundreds of thousands of Black Americans and members of the diaspora around the world came here four years ago to participate in the Year of Return.

"Your vision, Mr. President, made this possible. So, on behalf of all of those who have made the return, all those from America who join you tonight, and all those who will return in the future, thank you, Mr. President."[10]

Wearing a Monique Lhuillier white cape dress with minimal flower print, Vice President Harris, who is rarely spotted in caped dresses, went on to speak about Africa's relationship with the world and the paradigm shift that President Akufo-Addo called for during the 2022 Munich Security Conference. She called Ghana's leadership on the world stage vital and inspiring, recalling the historical celebration of Ghana's independence. "… [I]t inspired millions of Americans, as it did for millions around the world, including Reverend Dr. Martin Luther King, Jr., who came here to witness the dawn of a new era. Dr. King, as we all know, and he wrote, was deeply moved by what he saw here. He wrote and spoke of it for years after. He spoke and wrote about

Ghana President, US Vice President, First Lady of Ghana, and Second Gentlemen of US at Ghana State Dinner

what Ghana was teaching the world. And he predicted that Ghana's independence, and I will quote, 'will have world-wide implications and repercussions, not only for Africa, but for America.'"[11]

She said that the sentiment remains true today with Ghana becoming a leading voice for democracy around the world. "While we face real challenges, I look around tonight and I am truly more optimistic than ever. And I know that by working together, the United States and Ghana, alongside the diaspora and the people of this beautiful continent, will share our future for the better."[12]

At the conclusion of all remarks, dinner began. The press did not dine with the guests. We were sent to a holding area where they had prepared food for us. It wasn't as fancy as the food served to the invited guests, but there was jollof rice with some beef or chicken and vegetable options for people who were vegetarian. I love jollof rice, and to all the Nigerians reading this, I am unequivocally Team Ghana when it comes to jollof rice. I encourage you to lay down your arms and get on board.

I grew up eating Ghanaian food as much as I grew up eating American food as much as I grew up eating soul food as much as I grew up eating health-conscious California fusion cuisine. So, sitting in the Ghanaian palace, in that holding room, eating that jollof rice took me down memory lane.

Like Vice President Harris, my childhood took place at the intersection of two different cultures. She has talked and written about spending time with her Indian relatives and Jamaican relatives. She has traveled to visit or live with family in Canada, Jamaica, Zambia, and India. My father was born in 1950 into colonial Ghana under British rule. He grew up during the Pan-African movement, and he was only seven years old when Ghana declared its independence. He left home as a teenager after immigrating from Ghana to Texas in 1970. I cannot imagine what it must have felt like to leave the only home you've ever known and to travel to the United States at a time of incredible turmoil. The courage that my grandparents must have summoned to send their only son to the United States following the assassination of Martin Luther King Jr., Malcolm X, Medgar Evers, and so many folks who were fighting for freedom. The struggle for civil rights and for Black liberation in the United States wasn't divorced from the struggle for Black liberation in Ghana.

My mother grew up in Palmetto, Florida during the height of the civil rights movement. After segregation legally ended, in 1969, during her junior year, she remembers being bussed from Lincoln Memorial High School to Manatee High School in Bradenton, a formerly whites-only school. Manatee High School was established in 1897, so you can only imagine how tightly segregationists were clinging to Jim Crow as a way of life. As if the trauma of integration wasn't difficult enough, my mother remembers with profound sadness the day that Dr. Martin Luther King Jr. was assassinated. She was at a local drug store with her father when she saw a group of white kids celebrating his murder. Had it not been for my grandfather's intuition to leave at that very moment, who knows how those kids might have channeled their perversion. Still, on the other side of my mom's proximity to Black pain and struggle, there remains a deep abiding faith and cautious optimism based on how far we've come from the dark days of Jim Crow yet and still not far enough. In spite of the pain and struggle of Black people in this nation and abroad, my mom was very proud of her Black heritage, and my dad was very proud of his Ghanaian heritage. They both saw it as a source of resilience in what can be a cruel and unforgiving world to our people. They insisted on passing that pride along to me and my four older brothers. Each of the tribes throughout Ghana has its own traditions, and as descendants of the Ga tribe, my father closely followed Ga naming traditions. My parents ensured that each of us had a Ghanaian name, although I am the only member of the family without a Christian first name, including my parents.

One of the greatest gifts my parents gave me was a sense of belonging to a bloodline of courageous problem-solvers and innovators who worked to pass on a better world to the next generation. My mom and maternal grandmother, Addie Mae Thomas, shared stories with me about being the descendant of an enslaved great-great-grandfather called Bud who came from Byron about nineteen miles from Macon, Georgia. My maternal great-great-grandfather, John C. Thomas, was a farmer in Monticello, Florida who owned land that was passed down to my grandfather and his siblings. I remember being told that there was a cemetery somewhere in Georgia bearing the name of great-great-aunt Ollie Glover, a very fair skin woman who is said to have passed for being white. I have not yet fully corroborated this rich story and the circumstances of my family genealogy, so consider this my lost episode of PBS's *Finding Your Roots* for now.

It is a part of my story that is not radically different from that of other Black Americans whose ancestors were enslaved. So, when you see someone named Nii-Quartelai Quartey, you may want to stop and examine some of your assumptions before you comment on how well they speak English.

In Accra, my paternal grandfather, Rev. Prophet James Quartey, founded Quartey Memorial Secondary School. He noticed that many of the women in the area were not attending church services, and when he inquired why, they informed him that they did not have childcare for their younger children. To meet that need, my grandfather opened a nursery that eventually expanded into a K-8 school. My dad ensured that the history of the school was an inter-generational family service project and family business that stayed in our orbit even though we lived thousands of miles from those schoolhouse doors. My grandfather died before I was born, but through his service to the community and the school, I see his living legacy. I understand his love for his people, his commitment to people, and his demonstra-tion of his faith through his works. Still today, looking at our family crest on the school uniforms of present-day stu-dents brings me immense pride.

My dad shared a story with me about when he first came to America that I will never forget. He told me that he couldn't quite understand why it seemed that Black Americans were preoccupied with wanting to be seen. It was strange to him. Yet, after living here for some years, he began to understand the history of Black folks here, not just as a student, but through the eyes of my mom, and he began to see the pursuit of being seen differently. I believe he saw the troubling indignities of Black Americans that, sadly, have not waned fast enough still today.

An ocean apart, my paternal grandfather wasn't thrilled about my dad marrying my mom. My dad had commu-nicated to my grandfather that he was going to marry an American woman, and my own grandfather's perception at the time was that American women were lazy. He wanted my dad to marry a Ghanaian woman instead. It wasn't until after my parents were married and they made her first trip to Ghana together in 1977 that my grandfather had the chance to meet my mother for the first time. Being in her presence caused him to reexamine some of his underlying assumptions about American women. He saw that my mom could drive. He saw that my mom had a viewpoint upon the world and how dynamic she was. Meeting her challenged his preconceived notions about Black American women, and he began to see her differently. And if that was possible in the seventies for my grandfather, then I think it's possible for anybody reading this book who may have some preconceived notions about who the vice president is. I've never backed away from the opportunity to inspire and encourage people to test their assumptions because I've seen within my own family what is possible when folks have the courage to do so.

Think about the qualities of a good diplomat, being able to look beyond the surface, being able to communicate across cultures, having some regard for cultures and languages that are different from their own, being able to code switch, being multilingual (and I'm not just talking about language), having an appreciation for the history of different people, understanding power dynamics and what underlies those power dynamics. My multi-heritage household taught me all those things.

It also taught me the responsibility and occasional burden of being a bridge between cultures when you are American born. In some cases, you aren't Black enough. In some cases, you aren't immigrant enough. Your name is too American. Your name is too hard to pronounce.

Vice President Harris likely had to contend with similar criticisms. I have learned to be myself and, by extension, have an appreciation for different parts of different cultures. I see glimpses of that skill in Kamala, too—a skill that should be seen as a strength in a world leader.

I am American born and steeped in that history, but I am also of Ghanaian heritage and steeped in that as well. In some ways, my parents' world views complimented each other, and in other ways, their world views were sometimes at odds. My mom celebrated Black excellence, while my dad celebrated excellence that was inclusive of, but not exclusive to, Black excellence. I recall telling my dad about an invitation I received to write for a publication called *Black Voices* at the University of Southern California. It was a separate publication from the mainstream campus paper, but it was still a huge accomplishment in my mind. I could feel his pause through the phone line after I told him. Then, he communicated to me that I should strive to be the best and not just the best Black person. That was the type of clear message that I received from my dad my whole life. It never felt like a put-down of Black people. My dad was a proud graduate of an HBCU and a proud member of Kappa Alpha Psi® Fraternity. A Clarence Thomas sympathizer he absolutely was not. But he believed, in his heart of hearts, that I was capable of a transcendent level of leadership and he, in his own way, pushed me towards that. He helped me see myself as a citizen of the world beyond my heritage, which has allowed me to be a bridge across culture in my work. And I wonder if Kamala's immigrant mother had a similar effect on her.

As a kid, I witnessed both mom and dad do the cooking, maintain our home, pay bills, invest in promising enterprises, and occasionally organize family vacations. Both my parents worked. They worked hard. At one point, my dad worked day shift and my mom worked swing shift to ensure that there was a parent at home or nearby on a regular basis. I don't ever remember my parents hiring a babysitter. But, I recognize my good fortune in being exposed to both of their world views as it afforded me the ability to recognize how the beautiful variations of the African diaspora still carry the potential for interdependence.

Even in a society where copious amounts of information are at our fingertips, far too many people of all backgrounds do not understand the connection between Africa and Black Americans and its significance to the struggles that Black people still work to overcome today. Yet, we have one side of the political aisle that wants to ban books; erase Black history from US schools; and burn the ladder of opportunity that Diversity, Equity, and Inclusion initiatives are designed to facilitate. Thinking about this as I observed the legacy, the representation, and the absolute beauty of the state dinner, I felt even more compelled to ensure that historical insights like this become immortalized on the written page.

ESCAPING AMERICA

In 2019, the Ghanaian government launched its Year of Return campaign. Marking 400 years since the first enslaved

Africans reached America, the country invited African Americans, Afro-Caribbeans, and people of African descent anywhere in the world to return to the land of their ancestors.[13] Over half-a-million people answered the call and traveled en masse to Ghana in search of community; history; and for some, opportunity. Some stayed for a week, others stayed for a few months, and still others decided to give up their Western lives for Ghanaian citizenship. The initiative is considered one of the continent's most successful tourism campaigns, and in the years since, countries like Nigeria and Uganda have followed suit.

Watching from the outside, I had no clue about the level of cooperation that occurred between the Ghanaian government and the NAACP to make the Year of Return happen. Johnson explained that the Minister of Tourism for Ghana approached the organization in 2018 to talk about the potential for partnership. "At the same time, we were looking at how to expand our opportunity in terms of the NAACP Image Awards, looking at doing something like an Image Awards Africa." He said that while the NAACP was organizing a delegation of just under 300 people to commemorate the Year of Return, a group of celebrities was also organizing a return. "So, we decided to organize something between Christmas and New Year's, and it took off. It was a big party now."[14]

Black celebrities like Usher, Kendrick Lamar, Gabrielle Union, Boris Kodjoe, Nicole Ari Parker, and Chance the Rapper took part in the festivities. The annual Afrochella Music Festival took place at the same time, featuring musical artists from across the continent. Ghana found a way to link the richness of our ancestries, our search for belonging, our love for a good party, and our shared kinships across the diaspora with an incredibly important resource for African economic development: travel.

In 2022, the travel and tourism sector contributed 5.9 percent to Africa's gross domestic product, and that percentage is expected to continue growing.[15] This represents a real opportunity for the type of structural transformation that leads to economic diversification and stability.[16] The tourism industry offers African economies a rich financial source that is not dependent on the international demand for minerals and the continent's natural resources. Much like Dubai and the United Arab Emirates have done by diversifying their oil-rich economies into tourist hotspots, African tourism has potential for a comparable level of sustainable growth.

I talked with a US-African affairs expert who expressed their appreciation for the amazing job that some of the continent's Ministers of Tourism are doing to connect with the diaspora. "Particularly the diaspora that's in America," they said. "I think that on the positive end, there's hope. From the lens of an African American, I think there's optimism in the sense of reconnecting and understanding who one is and their culture." This person also sees it as an alternative way for people to flee the reality of America for many African Americans, "so you are starting to see more initiatives such as what Ghana is doing."[17]

The US-African affairs expert also brought up a point that I think is important as we seek to bridge the gaps between the reality of the continent and people's perceptions. Traveling to Africa is a costly endeavor, and it is cost-prohibitive for so many Black people in the United States. "You also still have to be able to afford it, so I think that the exposure and the ability to travel to places like Ghana, to travel to Africa from the perspective of African Americans, is still limited."[18]

They told me that the inability for some to see Africa for themselves may skew their perceptions and understanding of what is happening on the continent. Instead, they become rooted in a lot of stereotypes, false or incorrect notions about Africa that they receive from misinformation.

In 2020, to extend its Year of Return campaign, Ghana's government launched what it calls the Beyond the Return campaign.[19,20] With the theme, "A decade of African Renaissance—2020-2030," this ten-year project "seeks to create opportunities for people of African descent to connect with the Motherland through 7 Pillars."

1. **Experience Ghana** is the drive behind tourism to encourage "the Global African family to visit and experience Ghana."
2. **Invest in Ghana** focuses on creating business and land investment opportunities, along with easing the requirements for people of African descent to conduct business within the country.

3. **Diaspora Pathways** to Ghana concerns the legal and policy frameworks on visa acquisition (e-visa) and the potential institution of a diaspora visa. Pathway programs such as educational and work exchanges, work permits, and citizenship programs are also handled under this pillar.

4. **Celebrate Ghana** uses cultural festivals, media programs, and contemporary festivals to promote domestic tourism and create a sense of national consciousness.

5. **Brand Ghana** uses branding to promote a narrative of the country as a top travel destination and a "hub for the African renaissance."

6. **Give Back to Ghana** is designed to create ongoing legacies by fostering community service and giving. Initiatives like tree planting and community impact projects fall under this pillar.

7. **Promote Pan African Heritage and Innovation** focuses on Pan-Africanism and Ghanaian heritage by developing a pilgrimage tourism infrastructure around sites that were essential parts of the history of slavery in Ghana.[21,22]

21ST CENTURY PAN-AFRICANISM

David Maimela, founder and executive director of The Polisee Space, a Pan-African public policy consulting firm based in South Africa, wrote the following about the advancement of the Pan-African movement: "In order to advance the [P]an-African agenda we need to understand how the 21st century world works—how it includes and excludes others, how it presents opportunities whilst simultaneously threatening to recolonize the African continent. In order for this to happen we need, from across society, leading universities, leaders, countries and vibrant social movements that will provide critical and visionary leadership. All of this must be organized consciously into a formidable [P]an-African network that includes the African diaspora to reclaim [P]an-Africanism and Africa."[23]

The Ghanaian state dinner offered an incredible example of what this reclaiming of Pan-Africanism could look like in real time. There were Black American luminaries and African luminaries all in one room. These are Black folks who are leading democracies that are critically important to the future of the continent and the world. What other US vice president could have facilitated the magic in that room? Al Gore? Dick Cheney? Dan Quayle? Not even Vice President Biden. Their presence would not have the same impact, the same feelings. So, for the people who insist on denying Kamala's "Black girl magic"—on the basis of what? No other American vice president would have the credibility, the stature, code switching agility, or the aptitude to successfully pull off this type of trip.

There is the substance of being Black, the performance of being Black, and the politics of being Black. No leader is above critique, including Vice President Harris, but I suspect that a lot of the critique out there is incomplete. Some folks critique the vice president's performance, which is fine, but we cannot critique the performance and ignore the substance of what she is getting done. People critique the performance and the substance but ignore the politics that shape the environment she must work within. Because let's be real—sometimes the politics of a situation could care less about performance or substance. You can be pitch perfect, and the politics still are what they are. I think some critiques of the vice president are unfair. Some critiques of the vice president are gratuitous. Some critiques of the vice president are incomplete. It is time to balance out that equation.

CHAPTER THREE

A POWER RARELY EXPERIENCED

In 2021, the LGBTQ+ Rights Ghana Centre opened in Accra as a support hub for LGBTQ+ individuals living in the homeland of my father.[1] It offered services ranging from legal assistance and counseling to community awareness campaigns. But the primary function of the center was to provide a safe space for a group of marginalized people who are under constant threat of discrimination, harassment, or violence—a circumstance not so different from the experience of some members of the LGBTQ+ community in America.

Within weeks of opening, the police caved to condemnation from religious leaders and pressure from conservative politicians, shutting down this vital community hub. Citing concerns about public safety and violations of Ghanaian law, officials claimed that the organization promoted homosexual activities in opposition of Ghanaian cultural values.

Human rights advocates loudly condemned the closure and fought for the reopening of the center, which operates once again but under challenging conditions. The existence and closure of the LGBTQ+ Rights Ghana Centre serve as a stark reminder of the threats and uncertainty that beset members of the LGBTQ+ community in Ghana and other countries across the continent. This reality provided the backdrop to a routine press conference that unexpectedly evolved into an unforgettable moment in my life.

AN UNWAVERING RESPONSE

Arriving at the first joint press conference of the vice president's trip to Africa, there was some anticipation about what would be discussed. Both Vice President Harris and President Akufo-Addo of Ghana would deliver their respective comments and answer questions from both the US and Ghanaian press. As we often do, the press corps had gotten together ahead of time to trade notes about potential questions to ask. The entire press corps was allowed only four questions in total, and we wanted to make sure that each of them would be useful to the corps at large; so, I knew that one of the questions would center on anti-LGBTQ+ legislation moving through the Ghanaian parliament.

The vice president's prepared remarks highlighted the Biden administration's stated commitment to strengthening ties with African nations and advancing mutual interests.[2] She emphasized the importance of partnership and collaboration on vital issues like climate change and economic inequality.

Joint Press Conference with Vice President Kamala Harris of the US and President Akufo-Addo of Ghana

Her words also reiterated the interconnectedness of global issues and the need for collective action between African nations and the US to address those challenges. She spoke about economic development and the significance of trade as a driver of opportunity in both countries and underscored efforts by the Biden administration to promote investment and the development of infrastructure in Africa, speaking specifically of the Build Back Better World (B3W) partnership, a global infrastructure initiative launched by President Biden and G7 partners.[3] Vice President Harris's remarks emphasized the importance of private sector engagement and entrepreneurship to foster prosperity for all.

Climate change and environmental sustainability were also on the agenda for both Vice President Harris and President Akufo-Addo. Highlighting Ghana's strategic location, stable democracy, and growing economy, he made the argument for promoting investment and partnership. In addition to economic development and climate change, both Vice President Harris and President Akufo-Addo discussed the vital importance of protecting democratic principles and human rights across the continent of Africa, reaffirming each country's respective commitment to supporting democratic institutions and respecting fundamental freedoms through fair elections, free media, and government accountability.

Once the remarks were completed, President Akufo-Addo and Vice President Harris addressed inquiries from the Ghanaian press about investments and foreign policy. There were no surprises, and their answers essentially reiterated the commitments made during their prepared remarks. Next up, it was time for the American press corps to ask our questions. I felt an air of anticipation inside as *The New York Times* White House correspondent Zolan Kanno-Youngs walked to the microphone and prepared to ask a question that one or both of these world leaders would potentially shut down.

With a specific mention of a proposed Ghanaian bill that would imprison those engaging in same-sex intercourse, Zolan asked Vice President Harris about the trip's theme of collaboration and how that reconciled the Biden administration's commitment to calling out foreign governments that have advanced or proposed anti-gay legislation. Even before he completed his inquiry, members of the Ghanaian cabinet made their disapproval apparent. You could see their faces get tight and hear the whispers. You could even hear some laughter. Was it nervous laughter? Was it belittling laughter?

Was it somewhere in between? I don't know. But the immediate shift in energy was palpable.

Despite the angry stares and even some snickers from around the room, Vice President Harris never paused or hesitated in her response. Without missing a beat and standing tall with shoulders arched back, she said, "I'll start. I have raised this issue, and let me be clear about where we stand. First of all, for the American press who are here, you know that a great deal of work in my career has been to address human rights issues, equality issues across the board, including as it relates to the LGBTQ+ community. And I feel very strongly about the importance of supporting freedom and supporting and fighting for equality among all people, and that all people be treated equally. I will also say that this is an issue that we consider, and I consider to be a human rights issue, and that will not change."[4]

President Akufo-Addo's response looked vastly different from that of Vice President Harris's. "First of all, we don't have any such legislation here in Ghana," he declared sternly. "A bill has been proposed through the Parliament of Ghana, which has all kinds of ramifications, which is now being considered by the Parliament. It hasn't been passed. So, the statement that there is legislation in Ghana to that effect is not accurate. No legislation."

In hindsight, I believe that they both anticipated the question. You can tell when people are knocked off-kilter by a question, and they clearly were not. The Ghanaian president's response was essentially that the parliament will do what it wants to do, and let me school you on how this works here. It was his way of answering the question but not really answering the question.

In February 2024, the Ghanaian legislature passed the bill, paving the way for the imprisonment of anyone convicted of identifying as LGBTQ+ and a maximum five-year jail sentence for anyone forming or funding LGBTQ+ groups.[5] Passing of the legislation sparked an immediate Supreme Court challenge, which President Akufo-Addo gave as the reason for not signing the bill into law. But there is no denying the economic impact that this law could have on the country, including the potential loss of almost $4 billion in World Bank funding by 2030.[6]

It would've been easy for Vice President Harris to duck the question so as not to offend anyone in the room but at the expense of the freedom and dignity of a great many people outside the room. Ghana was the starting point, setting the tone for the entire trip ahead. By responding to the LGBTQ+ question honestly and basically doubling-down on her support of gay rights as human rights, she risked pulling focus from other aspects of the trip. What if folks on the continent decided to make this trip about her trying to persuade Africans into being more supportive of LGBTQ+ folks? She had some ambitious goals to achieve on the continent, particularly by not making the trip about humanitarian aid or public health but, instead, about entrepreneurship and investing more in the continent. Her objectives could have easily been derailed in that moment, but she took a stand anyway.

IN COMMUNITY WITH

Listening to the vice president's response, I felt surprised by her full-throated response but not surprised by her continued commitment to civil and human rights for all. I am very familiar with her lengthy track record of being in support of and in community with LGBTQ+ folks. Many years earlier, her first campaign consultant, Jim Rivaldo, worked on the campaign for gay rights trailblazer Harvey Milk, the first openly gay man to be elected to public office in California. Harris's campaign would be Rivaldo's last before passing away. After winning her first elected office as San Francisco district attorney in 2004, Vice President Harris established a hate crimes unit to investigate and prosecute anti-LGBTQ+ violence. In 2006, she organized a conference of over one hundred officials from across the country to discuss strategies to end the use of the so-called gay and transgender panic defenses. Thanks to her work, California became the first state to legally ban the practice in 2016, and in 2018, then senator Harris, along with other senators, introduced a bill to prohibit the practice nationally.

While serving as California's top prosecutor, she declined to defend in court California's Proposition 8 (a ballot measure that banned same-sex marriage in the state). And as one of the hopefuls for the 2020 Democratic presidential primary, her LGBTQ+ platform stood apart from the rest.

For me, it makes a material difference when you are not just in support of but in community with. Your allyship hits differently when you're in community with. I don't need you to take pity on me. I don't need you to support me as an act of charity, but I do need you to act in solidarity with me. I need you to understand that your humanity and my humanity are intertwined. Kamala Harris gets that. She understands the connection between the rights of all people, whether you are talking about women's reproductive rights, LGBTQ+ rights, or racial justice. And, in a lot of ways, she is far ahead of her peers—not just in her understanding but in her decision to use her platform, her bully pulpit, to act in the public interest when it comes to communities on the margin. I witnessed that on full display in Africa.

A big part of allyship, in my view, involves risking something, and I saw that from the vice president in a way that you don't always see from Black folks in general, particularly those of her generation and older. She put her credibility on the line with African leaders, taking the risk that they would view her as a tool of the West instead of a bridge between the West and Africa. For those who share in her belief, how she showed up is really no surprise. But if you are disturbed by her response, if you're on that tolerance kick of "Well, I'll tolerate your marriages, but I don't think it's a one for one," then the power of her response will not resonate with you because you would rather her not give voice to the people to whom she gave a voice in such a powerful way.

When there are people who talk about the vice president as ineffective and over her skis—some of which are Black people—part of what they are objecting to is her actual and perceived identity politics. If your worldview is not such where diversity is seen as strength and unity as a source of power, it'll be hard to see her as anything more than a threat to the values of those already in power. Vice President Harris leans into her entire identity as a strength, not as something that needs to be concealed or managed, which is a different way of showing up and engaging as a world leader. So, for folks who see her identity as a weapon and think leaning into your race is "playing the race card," she feels like a threat. And there are a lot of people in positions of power, influence, and authority who see her that way before she even opens her mouth. It's out there in the narrative around her, in between the sentences and paragraphs of what's written and said. We need to understand that reality as we opine on those narratives and the motives behind them. Now, I am not suggesting that the vice president walks on water, but I am suggesting that she represents a politic that has not yet peaked in popularity.

THE PLURALITY OF BLACK LIBERATION

If you ask Black women if their experience differs from that of white women, it's likely they'll tell you that it absolutely does—in some cases vastly. And historically, we know that to be the truth. Think about the Nineteenth Amendment and the willingness of suffragists to exclude Black women from participating in the right for women to vote. Think about the fact that it took Black women until the 1960s to get that right on paper. This is just one example of how, not just racism, but white supremacy can play out just among women. The same is true among LGBTQ+ folks.

When you look at the people who have historically led LGBTQ+ legacy organizations, consider the work that looms large in terms of advancing racial equity. While we rightfully advance our valiant pursuit of full equality, we cannot do so at the expense of racial equity, yet there are still too many examples where the experiences of Black LGBTQ+ folks vastly differ from those of white LGBTQ+ folks. Think about the history of HIV/AIDS and who had access to resources and therapies early in the movement. Spoiler alert: It wasn't Black folk, hence, the stark disparities we still must overcome. During the 2022 US monkeypox outbreak, barriers existed for Black people in terms of education and access to getting the vaccine. Though I think there's more of a consciousness around these racial disparities now, my generation is no different. Yes, there are more people in positions of power, influence, and authority to talk more openly about it, but we still have a long way to go when dealing with the legacy of white supremacy that attacks us outside the Black community. But exponentially more painful, the legacy of white supremacy that attacks us from inside the Black community.

Issa Rae got folks rooting for everybody Black. People are saying the quiet part out loud, and I fully support us rooting for us. But is it a singular us or is it the plural us? I've found that, in practice, a lot of people are really referring to the singular us. In other words, the people who look like us, love like us, and live like us. The plural us makes room for a longer table, a longer range, a wider range of Black people, Black thought, and Black experiences. And I don't think we can call ourselves serious champions of Black liberation if we are not in the business of building a longer table and making room for a wider range of Black thought and experiences that even go beyond the United States from across the diaspora.

People who are Black and queer and those who are allies of Black queer people hear only part of the story. We rarely see public and powerful demonstrations of solidarity and allyship support, love, or joy. For us, that allyship comes with the white gaze where folks root for everybody Black with an asterisk that says "except for Black and queer" or "except for Black and transgender." The fight for Black liberation recognizes, quite simply, that nobody's free until all of us are free, but the questions become "What is our operational definition of 'all of us'? What is our operational definition of 'freedom'?" In the Netflix documentary *What Happened, Miss Simone?* the late great Nina Simone said, "I'll tell you what freedom is to me: no fear." I couldn't agree more.

If "all of us" does not include people who have a Black trans experience; if "all of us" does not include Black women, if "all of us" doesn't include Black queer people; if "all of us" doesn't include Black men; if "all of us" does not include Black folks who don't speak English; if "all of us" doesn't include Black folks who are disabled; if "all of us" does not include Black people with and without college degrees; if "all of us" does not include Black people whose experiences may be different from ours, then we cannot call ourselves champions of Black liberation. More accurately, we might refer to it as the liberation of people like ourselves. Keep Black liberation out of your mouth if your operational definition of Black is singular and not as plural, vast, and wide as it needs to be for a time such as this.

AN OUTSTRETCHED HAND?

Arriving in Ghana, I felt a consuming sense of warmth, an embrace, an outstretched hand for Black people to visit. But, for some of us, that outstretched hand is coupled with a left hook simply based upon the other aspects of our identities. I took on a life-changing assignment to Africa in the protective bubble of the vice president of the United States where my welfare was not at all a concern, but would I feel the same level of safety outside this protective bubble if traveling with my husband?

In my interview with Rashad Robinson from Color of Change, he discussed his experience of traveling to Ghana with his partner and his concerns for their safety. "I didn't know if I'd be the only queer person on the delegation. But I knew that if I wasn't, I would probably be the person whose activism in service of LGBT people was certainly most prominent."[7] He said that he spoke with some folks at the US Embassy in Ghana before embarking on the trip as well as after arriving, noting that the US ambassador went out of her way to sit next to and converse with him and his partner during the trip events.

Robinson also shared his perspective on the anti-LGBTQ Ghanaian bill. "This type of legislation exists inside of a culture that can oftentimes be unsafe, can make people feel like they have to be silent... I lead a Black civil rights organization. That's not an LGBT organization, but I believe Black people exist in all sorts of forms and bodies. And that's the type of organization I'm going to lead. They want to take from our culture, our brilliance, and our contributions, and then remain silent when we're under attack." He shared some insight into the economic implications of the legislation in a country where the 2023 gross domestic product represented only 0.03 percent of the world economy.[8] "This type of law stands in the way of possibilities for opportunity. And I do think that with the next big kind of corporate engagement around bringing Black people to Ghana, we'll have to have very clear questions about what we mean when we say 'Black.'"[9]

Human Rights Watch lists Ghana's treatment of the LGBTQ+ community as mixed. Section 104(1)(b) of Ghana's Criminal Offences Act criminalizes "unnatural carnal knowledge" defined as "penile penetration of anything other than a vagina." While this holdover from colonial rule is rarely enforced, the safety and rights of LGBTQ+ people in Ghana are constantly at risk. They commonly face physical and psychological violence in their daily lives and systematic violence as discriminatory bills are introduced in the legislature. The stigma is loud and incorrigible. Derogatory terms are commonly used in public spaces without apology, and members of the LGBTQ+ community report violence perpetrated by family members if their sexual orientation is even suspected. Fears of family rejection drive people to live double lives in order to stay safe; some even enter into heterosexual marriages for the sole purpose of keeping themselves safe. Acts of violence against LGBTQ+ people commonly go unreported out of fear of being outed or arrested themselves.

In 2022, a report by Open Democracy found that Ghanaian doctors promoted "conversion therapy" practices at a workshop for medical professionals.[10] The event was organized by the National Coalition for Proper Human Sexual Rights and Family Values, an anti-LGBTIQ+ campaign group in Ghana that backs anti-LGBTQ+ legislation. One of their proposed bills would have required the reporting of LGBTQ+ people to the authorities and compelled conversion therapy. While the bill was unsuccessful, it demonstrates the constant legal threat that exists for the LGBTQ+ community in Ghana.

And these threats are in no way limited to Ghana. As of 2023, homosexuality was outlawed in more than thirty African nations.[11] In the same month that Vice President Harris stood up for LGBTQ+ rights in Ghana, the country of Uganda passed a law making it a crime to identify as LGBTQ+. The penalties are severe, including death or life in prison. In 2014, the Same Sex Marriage (Prohibition) Act, banning all gay relationships, was signed into Nigerian law.[12] In the northern states that have adopted Shari'a law, the punishment is death by stoning.[13] Three men were sentenced to death by stoning in 2022 after being convicted of engaging in homosexual activities by an Islamic sharia court. In southern Nigeria, under the secular criminal code, the maximum punishment is sixteen years of imprisonment.

Much of the anti-LGBTQ+ legislation in Africa is influenced by European colonial rule and does not reflect the traditional laws of African tribal nations.[14] Europeans looked down upon the traditional sexualities of African people, portraying them as evidence of their alleged racial inferiority, and anti-gay legislation was another tool of their oppression. Today, we know that many denominations of Christianity condemn homosexuality, and unfortunately, millions of Africans are susceptible to those hateful teachings. The thread of colonialism runs through African politics and colors in the way we examine LGBTQ+ rights on the continent. It creates a distortion that the rights of some are more important than the rights of others, and that bolsters a school of thought that makes my love for my husband wrong. There's that saying that it takes a village to raise a child. Well, the village consists of all sorts of people. White supremacy casts a distorted view of our fellow villagers.

To be fair, there are positive actions being taken on the continent in recognizing the human rights of LGBTQ+ people. In 2006, South Africa became the first country in Africa and only the fifth country globally to legalize same-sex marriages, giving couples both constitutional and statutory protections.[15] In 2015, Mozambique did away with a colonial-era code that defined same-sex relationships as "vices against nature." In 2019, Botswana's High Court decriminalized both male and female same-sex relationships by replacing a British-instituted law that had been in place since 1965. The Supreme Court of Namibia issued a ruling in 2013 that foreign same-sex marriages must be recognized as being equal to heterosexual marriages.

A lot of gay folks feel comfortable traveling to South Africa because of the protections guaranteed under their constitution, but what about the other fifty-three countries of Africa? I cannot travel to the majority of them with my husband for the fear that we might attract unwanted attention from folks who might seek to do us harm or over-zealous law enforcement. Seven African nations were included on the "Forbes Travel Safety Report: 20 Worst Places For Gay Travelers In 2021."[16] It is a reality that I cannot shake, and I say this as a Black gay man who passes for being heterosexual, if you will. You would not necessarily know that I am gay when I walk in the room. Not by design. It's just who I am. But there are a lot of people in my community who don't pass, and they are as entitled to their human rights as everyone else. It is heart-wrenching to realize that Mother Africa, who is pregnant with so much potential, may be losing or squandering some of that potential because people who are leading that innovation and creativity may be LGBTQ+ and not afforded the basic protections that allow them to bring their full selves to the work of powering Africa's future.

Simply Love

During my graduate studies in Ghana, I met a village leader named King Peggy, author of *King Peggy: An American*

Secretary, Her Royal Destiny, and the Inspiring Story of How She Changed an African Village. I asked how she and her people reconciled their Christian belief in God with their recognition and worship of the deities that existed in their culture. She explained to me that it really is not difficult at all because they view those deities as God's little helpers. So, it is not as conflicting as some in the West would have folks believe. That conversation opened up the space for me to lean into a counter-narrative about the possibility that different people who speak different languages and carry different beliefs, who worship God but call upon God's little helpers on other matters, may also be able to accept LGBTQ+ people. No big deal.

For a long time, many Native American tribes have understood this concept of being two-spirit people, having both masculine and feminine energy. So, what folks who are gender-nonconforming are communicating may be revolutionary to Main Street Americans, but there are Native Americans who have been leaning into this for a long time. My Ghanaian grandmother's native languages were Ga and Twi. Still to my knowledge, there are few to no words for "gay" in either of those languages. And if there is no word for it in a native tongue that dates back even further than the modern boundaries of the country—before Christianity was introduced—then maybe it does not matter as much as those who continuously push anti-LGBTQ+ narratives would have us believe. Maybe it is a demonstration of humanity that has existed since the beginning of time—a demonstration that I felt in the vice president's response to Zolan's question during the Ghanaian press conference. I remember seeing men walking down the street hand-in-hand during my first trip to Ghana. I was told that it was simply a showing of friendship, not a declaration of an identity, and while I accepted that explanation, I knew there was a deeper takeaway. Those men walking down the street together loved one another. That's all. It was simply love. No fear.

CHAPTER FOUR

THE CREATIVE ECONOMY

My Ghanaian father attended college on scholarship at a small HBCU in Tyler, Texas. One day, some of his buddies came running up to his dorm room, excitedly banging on his door, exclaiming that his people were on the television. Curious and confused, he followed them down to the student lounge to see what they were talking about. Imagine his shock, disappointment, and disgust to see images of Tarzan and Jane playing on a black and white television. It sounds ridiculous, but that was the level of understanding that even some Black Americans had about life in Africa at the time. Until very recently, images of jungles, poverty, famine, and corruption shaped many people's warped assumptions about the continent of Africa. Even in my own childhood, to see more accurate representations of African life, I had to wait for family members to visit Ghana and bring back VHS and BETA tapes of African movies.

So, when the vice president pulled up to Vibrate recording studio, a collaborative workplace for young creatives in Ghana, my heart jumped at the thought of centering a side of the country not often celebrated. I was even more excited to see Sheryl Lee Ralph and Idris Elba standing outside of the facility, waiting to greet us. Their presence showcased international collaboration and the infinite possibilities of Africa's creative economy.

HIGH VIBRATIONS

Approaching the Vibrate studio, I had no idea what to expect inside of the bright yellow walls covered in names like Kendrick Lamar and Virgil Abloh. There was also a skateboard park in the back, and I remember thinking, "Okay, this is different." I don't think a lot of folks in the US would expect to see a place like this existing in Accra. Many people tend to view the creative economy through the lens of America with Hollywood, New York City, and increasingly Atlanta standing as the beacons of creativity. Over the last few decades, more people around the world have embraced Bollywood in India, and in recent years, Nollywood in Nigeria, but being at Vibrate studio opened my eyes to the incredible potential of this largely untapped market. Some places claim to be creative spaces. Well, Vibrate studio felt like a creative space. Composed of a community recording music studio and music business program, Vibrate is designed to assist emerging musicians and music entrepreneurs with the tools and skills they need to succeed in the global music market. Walking through, I was impressed by the level of equipment and technologies within the space, and I could almost feel the creative energy in the air. Vibrate was on-brand with a whole vibe you could not ignore.

The vice president's brief remarks centered on the universal language of music and artistry. "You are speaking in a way that, around the globe, people hear songs that are rooted in concepts like freedom and individuality and self-determination," she said. "This is the work you each are doing. And so I feel so honored and privileged to be here and to thank you for all of the creative work. It takes a lot of courage, it takes a lot of sacrifice to be an artist, but the work that is happening here is influencing and bringing joy to people around the world."[1]

Vice President Harris ended by introducing Elba and Ralph, whom she referred to as some friends she brought with her. Having these two very distinguished Black artists there to pour into this experience and encourage these young artists was an impactful reminder to folks inside and outside of the room how much opportunity exists on the continent. "I'm so happy to share with all of you here, at the invitation of Vice President Kamala Harris," said Ralph after serenading the crowd with her incredible voice, "that it is in spaces like this that artists find their voices, perfect their art, so that they are able to bring it out to the world. And we are very happy to be here with you today as we support each of you in your individual art." She shared that it had been a hard journey for her and will be a hard journey for the young artists in the room. "But as artists, we never let the difficulty stop us because it is what we must do."

Nii-Quartelai Conducts On-the-Fly Interview with US Actor Idris Elba

Elba spoke next, thanking the vice president for bringing them all together in the Vibrate studio space. "The creative industry has so many opportunities…it is part of our culture, our identity, and it has yet to be explored in a major way." He called the trip a step in the right direction. "But don't forget that it starts with you. It starts with hard work. It starts with places like this. It starts with supporting places like this so that we can see more talent grow and come through places like this with more entrepreneurialism and more innovation."

I had a chance to interview Elba afterwards for a little bit, and one of the things that struck me about our conversation was insights about his own investments in producing films on the continent. So, here is this big international star who is saying to people, "Come join me and invest in the continent." There is so much opportunity for Black Hollywood to

Idris Elba, Sheryl Lee Ralph, and Vice President Kamala Harris at Vibrate in Ghana

lean into. Yes, we know that Black Hollywood may not have the same money as Hollywood at large, but we also know that our dollars go really far on the continent. So, it's going to be interesting to see whether Black Hollywood responds to that call to action from people like Elba and Ralph. Imagine how many Tyler Perry Studios there could be in places like Ghana and other countries across the continent with even a modest investment. The idea leads back to a major theme of the vice president's trip—investing more in African entrepreneurship.

Ralph also shared with me some thoughts about the importance of viewing Africa as a major global player when it comes to supporting the next generation of Black content creators. "Africa is a rich cultural tapestry with a burgeoning population," she said. "Ignoring Africa in supporting the next generation of Black content creators would sadly close the door to a diverse and talented pool of creators. Additionally, Africa's growing digital infrastructure and connectivity provide a platform for content dissemination, making it a crucial player in the global creative landscape." Having both Elba and Ralph present at the Vibrate studio really put an emphasis on the opportunities that abound among the creative community in Ghana and across the continent.

THE COINS

The contributions of artists, creators, and innovators ripple through our lives, shaping culture, sparking imagination, and fostering connections. Filmmakers transport us to places we never knew existed and provide us with the intimate moments that are etched into our memories. Musicians soothe our worries with melodies of love, loss, joy, and resilience that resonate across generations. Designers mold aesthetics into tangible forms that we use to decorate our bodies, our homes, and the way we show up in the world. Writers spin words into beautiful patchworks that can comfort and disturb us at the same time. And in a book about the Motherland, we absolutely cannot leave out the craftspeople—those potters and weavers who turn raw materials into exquisite creations that symbolize culture and identity.

The creatives among us bring beauty and depth into our daily lives, but they also bring coins into the economy. In the United States alone, arts and culture employment generated more than $446 billion in wages in 2020, and the economic output of creative economy sectors amounted to $877 billion, which includes a $28-billion trade surplus from the export of artistic and cultural goods and services like movies and video games. In 2020, arts and cultural economic activity accounted for 4.2 percent of America's gross domestic product (GDP) and its future valuation is trillions.[2] What impact would it have if we started to think about the creative economy in Africa the same way we think about the creative economy in the United States?

Africa's creative economy has been steadily gaining momentum in recent years, evolving into a global force. With the global popularity of Afrobeats, a growing film industry, and sought-after designers, the continent's creative economy generates an average of $4.2 billion annually and employs half a million people in its cultural goods market alone. The first-ever Creative Africa Nexus Summit was held in December 2021 to showcase Africans leveraging what was described as "CreaTech" where creativity meets technology.[3] Creative Africa Nexus is an initiative of the African Export-Import Bank established to support creative economy entrepreneurs across the continent. The event gave folks the opportunity to talk with industry leaders from all over the world about monetizing their talents while also discussing the impediments that keep the African film industry largely untapped.

A 2021 reporting by the United Nations Educational, Scientific and Cultural Organization (UNESCO) explored the untapped potential of Africa's film industry.[4] *The*

African Film Industry: Trends, Challenges and Opportunities for Growth provided the first-ever mapping of the continent's film-making sector, which at the time, accounted for $5 billion in GDP.[5] But according to the UNESCO report, Africa's film and audiovisual industries have the potential to create more than 20 million jobs and contribute over $20 billion in GDP. While growth has been steady, evidenced by the fact that Nigeria produces about 2,500 films each year, much of this creative economy goes undiscovered due to some systematic roadblocks. For example, as of the 2021 UNESCO report, the continent of Africa had only one cinema screen per 787,402 people. In addition, piracy remains a major issue with estimates that between 50 and 75 percent of potential revenue is lost due to these acts of theft.

Content piracy is the modern face of art theft, misappropriating the work of creative folks without fairly compensating them for it. A lot of people refer to it as a victimless crime, but unchecked piracy can destroy the potential of Africa's creative economy. It's been reported that digital video piracy costs the US economy more than half a million industry jobs each year and up to $29.2 billion in lost revenue.[6] If the impact is that large in a country with anti-piracy laws and systems in place, imagine the impact it has in Africa where so many creatives work without the benefit of any national regulations.

South Africa and Nigeria are leading the way in shaping Africa's creative economy in areas of film. According to the PwC Global Entertainment & Media Outlook, Nigeria's media and entertainment industry is among the world's fastest-growing creative sectors, which puts its media industry on-track to become a significant export for the country.

Part of that success comes from the country's willingness to address digital piracy and the protection of intellectual property. During the same month of the vice president's visit to the continent, Nigerian president Muhammadu Buhari signed the Copyright Act 2022 into law, which aims to ensure fair recognition for intellectual efforts, facilitate compliance with international copyright treaties and conventions, and enforce effective regulation and enforcement of laws by the Nigerian Copyright Commission.[7] These legal measures recognize the value of Nigeria's creative economy as something worth protecting.

Netflix became involved in the Nigerian film industry in 2020, injecting about $23 million. While this level of investment is noteworthy, it accounts for only about 13 percent of the $175 million that Netflix invested into the sub-Saharan Africa film industry between 2016 and 2022. The vast majority of that money—about $125 million (71 percent)—went to South Africa's film industry, which is the most profitable on the continent.

South Africa is heavily invested in its film industry. The country far exceeds the continental average with approximately 800 cinema screens across more than seventy theaters.[8] It also maintains several pieces of legislation against digital piracy and copyright infringement. Cape Town Film Studios is a $35-million, state-of-the art complex that has become a filming location for some of the world's top filmmakers.[9] Experts suggest that, with the right infrastructure and investment, the untapped potential of South Africa's film industry could reach more than \$8.04 billion.[10]

If African countries like Ghana follow these examples into the creative economic spaces, it could have a multitude of benefits for their economic development. The creative economy can empower local artists and artisans to earn sustainable incomes through their talents and gifts, which will be particularly impactful for the continent's younger generations who will soon account for a significant percentage of the world's population. It enhances tourism, attracting visitors from all over the world who yearn to personally experience the rich cultural heritage of the African countries. A thriving creative economy has the potential to substantially grow and diversify national economies while also celebrating the many rich cultures of the continent.

A TRUTHFUL NARRATIVE

When most Westerners think of Africa, their thoughts typically go to one of two things: images of starving children, poverty, corruption, and coups or videos they have seen of lions chasing zebras across the savannah. This is because the mainstream narratives surrounding Africa have long been shaped by external perspectives that are often oversimplified and skewed in a direction that perpetuates an indifferent view of Africa.

Now, I am not suggesting that poverty and wildlife are not part of the continent's narrative because they absolutely are. But limiting the view to such a small scope not only does a disservice to the incredible diversity of the continent but also to Black people across the diaspora who may never be introduced to the greatness from which they came.

A Western gaze has long cast Africa as a land of perpetual struggle, a place that needed saving. It reduces a complex continent to simplistic stereotypes, perpetuating a narrative that neither reflects the full spectrum of African life nor acknowledges its resilience of African people in overcoming the Western colonialism and theft that has pilfered so much of the continent's resources. Even today, some people still think about the entire continent of Africa as a single country. Throughout my entire life, I have had people ask me "Your family is from Africa?" as if Africa is the size of the state of Connecticut. I've heard people refer to items or traditions as "African" with zero understanding that the continent has different regions, fifty-four countries, and many tribal identities. People do not conflate England with France or Swedes with Hungarians. These countries have different histories, traditions, and origin stories. The same is true across the continent of Africa.

Erasing this monochromatic lens requires embracing the authenticity of African countries and highlighting the dynamic landscape of innovation and cultural creativity.

That's the importance of uplifting the continent's creative economy. The world needs to see real stories in order to flip the prevailing script and reveal a vibrant Africa that defies the widely-held assumptions.

We see glimpses of a global celebration of African artistry in the popularity of Afrobeats, a music genre that has exploded over the last five years. While some folks argue that Afrobeats was influenced by hip-hop, others argue that the tribal drums and African music actually inspired hip-hop. Then, there is a third camp that views Afrobeats as a full-circle moment demonstrating the cross-influence of Pan-Africanism. For me, African music was always part of my childhood. On Saturday mornings, the household stereo woke us all up with a mixture of soul and Ghanaian Highlife music. It was our cue to get up and clean up. As much as soul and R&B music were a part of my childhood's soundtrack, so was Highlife music. So, when I hear Afrobeats, my mind goes back to those days, and it is fascinating to me that my dad's music is now mainstream. Folks younger than I are all about this music that I asked my dad to turn down as a kid when my friends came over to our house to visit.

I recall attending an event at the Howard University Center for Journalism & Democracy Summit hosted by its founder, Nikole Hannah-Jones, author of *The 1619 Project*. Throughout the day, she repeatedly reminded us that narrative drives policy. Narrative drives policy. This trip was an incredible opportunity to change the narrative about African nations. So, it's not just when you know better, you do better, but when you know better, you change the narrative. And by changing the narrative, it allows for better policy; better policy can allow for more opportunity for economic justice. Disrupting the legacies of colonialism across the diaspora starts with asking what stories are we telling ourselves? What stories are we telling our communities?

What story are we telling the world? And who is that story serving? Far too often, the narratives coming out of the continent haven't served the people but have served the narrow self-interest of folks that have sought to have their way with the people and resources of Africa.

With authentic narratives, we can hear the true voices of activists fighting for LGBTQ+ rights in Accra and see through the creative lens of the young people at the Vibrate studio. Africa's creative economy will play a pivotal role in shaping these narratives. Journalists, filmmakers, musicians, craftspeople, and writers can all show the world the multifaceted realities and promise of Africa.

AHEAD OF THE CURVE

The intentionality of the vice president's team in showcasing a well-rounded view of the continent really struck me. They took us off the beaten path of what a diplomatic trip typically looks like to destinations and experiences that made us think about the perceptions, realities, and potential of Africa. I felt like more than an observer of the cultures and histories. At times, I felt immersed in them and gob-smacked by the unrealized potential. Vice President Harris's team even produced a soundtrack for all to enjoy by creating a Spotify playlist featuring Afrobeats artists. They didn't wait for the Grammys to affirm this incredible musical genre; they said, "Here's some really cool music coming out of Ghana, coming out of Nigeria, coming out of the continent." That's how much they leaned into this trip and how intentional they were about exposing, not just the press corps and other participants, but the whole world to a richer African narrative than what my dad's classmates had been exposed to in the early 1970s. In hindsight, it turns out that Kamala was ahead of the curve. Almost a year later at the 66th Annual Grammy Awards, I couldn't have guessed I would be on assignment to witness Burna Boy deliver the first Afrobeats performance after Tyla won the first ever Grammy for Best African Music performance.

The vice president used her global platform to challenge folks' assumptions about Africa, and she continues to do so. In September 2023, six months after the trip, she collaborated with the Recording Academy's Black Music Collective to honor the fiftieth anniversary of hip-hop, and her experience on the continent showed up in her remarks.

"Today, hip-hop is everywhere. So, as [v]ice [p]resident of the United States, I have traveled this world and I firmly believe hip-hop is one of America's greatest exports," she said. "In fact, earlier this year, I was in Ghana, joined by some friends like Idris Elba and Sheryl Lee Ralph and Spike Lee. And I visited a recording studio where young artists, influenced by hip-hop, have helped to create their own unique music: the globe-trotting Afrobeats. And the same is happening around the world where young people have adopted hip-hop to tell their own stories of self-determination. From the streets of Ghana to France, to Japan, to Brazil, and to its home all the way back in the Bronx, hip-hop is traveling the world."[11]

If folks open their ears and listen, they just might be surprised at how seamlessly Kamala is able to connect the dots in terms of lived experiences and opportunities for Black folks across the diaspora. Technology has become a game-changer for presenting a narrative of the continent rarely seen before. Thanks to this thing called the internet, we no longer have to wait for our family members or loved ones to come back from the continent bearing video tapes to see a truthful picture of African countries. Streaming platforms are embracing content that is more reflective of various African experiences across the diaspora, and for many of us, those images are far different from the ones we carried around in our heads. They challenged some of our underlying assumptions. Today, you would have to be completely disconnected or willfully ignorant to view Africa as the land of Tarzan and Jane.

But this is not only an entertainment strategy; it can also be a news strategy. What does it look like to set up a news bureau in different parts of Africa? We are in a time when everyone is warring for eyeballs—this digital transformation of entertainment, news, and information where everyone competes to attract the most viewers, the most engagement, and the most consumers. To what extent are folks on the continent a part of that equation, a part of that business case? As Vice President Harris pointed out at the very start of the trip, one in four people on the planet earth will reside on this continent by 2050. There can't just be national security and foreign policy implications in that reality. There are also implications in terms of the business case for global investments. What attracts investment? Good governance, security, talent, and infrastructure. So, there's a role for the government to play when it comes to investment on the continent of Africa, but there's also a role for the private sector to play. And it's going to be interesting to see what industries decide to lean in. It's great to see folks like Elba and Ralph using their platform to attract attention and investment. But when are Warner Bros. Discovery, Paramount, FOX, and others going to answer the call?

CHAPTER FIVE

THAT'S WHAT WENT VIRAL?

Though my trip to Cape Coast Castle as part of the vice president's press corps was not my first time visiting, being there stirred up some deep emotions within me. An ever-present stench remains within those walls, a haunting that is omnipresent. Years earlier, while doing graduate work at Pepperdine University, I had traveled to Ghana and was taken to Cape Coast Castle, and the memory of that smell rushed back to me. I remember learning that Cape Coast Castle was built on an ancient burial ground for the Fante people. Colonizers literally built this castle of horror on top of sacred ground. Visiting this site left me with a painful realization about the perversion of slavery; that added insult to injury. We talk a lot about the tragedy and the trauma of the slave trade. What we don't talk enough about is the perversion of it that still impacts our lives. Book bans exemplify how that perversion permeates our society in real time. Officials at our highest levels of state government are leading this renewed resistance to telling a Black history that actually centers the voices of Black people. The hallmark of white supremacy is perversion and distraction from the truth. Cape Coast Castle stands as an incredible monument to that reality.

A PAINFUL PAST

Cape Coast Castle dates back to 1555 when Portuguese traders erected a trading lodge called Cabo Corso.[1] The Swedes took it over and built a fort in 1653. The European nations wanted the land because of its sheltered beaches and proximity to Elmina Castle (now called St. George's Castle), another painful vestige of colonialism erected by the Portuguese to protect gold trades.[2] Control of the land meant an advantage in the marketplace, and the countries fought for that control. It was eventually captured by the Danes with help from the local Fetu chief.[3] A few years later, a British fleet conquered the fort and expanded upon the existing lodge to build the castle. The merchants formed alliances with tribal political leaders in the area, and a town eventually grew around the castle. Forced sexual relations between European men and African women led to a significant biracial population.[4] These people were allowed to learn skilled trades and serve in military type units, but they also provided the bridge of trust that Europeans needed to ensure a continuous supply of African commodities, including the African people. As the supply of slave cargos grew into a larger segment of their profits, the castle was expanded again with forts that could hold more captives. The number of enslaved people that could be processed through Cape Coast Castle made it a major part of the Transatlantic Slave Trade.

After being forcibly marched to the castle, captive Africans were examined and judged fit or unfit for sale. Being deemed fit meant a chest branding with a hot iron, a practice done to prevent African traders from switching healthy enslaved people who had been bought for unfit ones.[5] The horrendous conditions of the castle's underground dungeons starkly differed from the luxurious living conditions of the castle above. Thousands of enslaved Africans were warehoused at Cape Coast Castle in terrifying darkness with death and illness all around them. Those who didn't die from malaria or yellow fever would eventually be assembled within the interior courtyard. Having been shackled in the dungeons for months at a time, the sunlight must have burned their eyes as they were led through the Door of No Return, a passageway to the beach where slave vessels waited to take them on a horrendous voyage.

Arriving to the castle site by helicopter as part of the vice president's press corps was a surreal experience. I could barely hear my own thoughts over the noise of the spinning blades. But as I looked down over that sacred piece of history, I was deeply moved and humbled as if the spirit of my father was with me. Here I was, a full-fledged adult, a full-fledged professional journalist traveling back to the place of his birth, but I don't think he ever got to experience his homeland from that perch. In Dr. Martin Luther King Jr.'s "I've Been to the Mountaintop" speech, he said, "… I've seen the Promised Land. I may not get there with you. But I want you to know

Vice President Harris at Door of Return in Ghana

tonight, that we, as a people, will get to the Promised Land."
It felt like that moment for me. My deceased father may not
have been there with me to physically share in that experience, but I definitely felt his presence from the other side
on that noisy US military helicopter. And that was a deeply
humbling feeling, a deeply moving experience for me.

There was also the weight of responsibility that came from
traveling with the press corps on a historic trip with a historic
vice president. I wondered what the ancestors were thinking.
Were they rejoicing that someone who shared their bloodline
had made such a grand return to shine a light on the horror,
the inhumanity, the injustice that took place on that sacred
land? What a stunning, yet cautionary, tale to the world about
the history that was made there, ironically, at a time when
there are forces out there that would pedal in revisionist history, trying to sanitize and erase this history. And so, I thought

Nii-Quartelai in Transit to Cape Coast Castle on Military Helicopter in Ghana

it was an incredible act of resistance, quite frankly, by this vice president to show up there in the way that she did and to be as vulnerable as she was willing to be. Something that, in my view, has been a challenge for her as an elected official.

Having experienced Cape Coast Castle before, I wasn't as emotionally moved as some other members of the press

Nii-Quartelai and Aerial View of Black Star Square Ahead of Vice President Harris's Speech in Ghana

corps. But it served as an important reminder of what's possible when human beings are allowed to succumb to their worst impulses. Somebody actually thought up this castle of torture. This is a really important point to make. It did not just pop up out of nowhere. Somebody actually thought up a way to systematically create the trafficking business of its

Nii-Quartelai, Eugene Daniels, and Zolan Kanno-Young
at Cape Coast Castle in Ghana

time. And we can't be so removed from history where we think that that kind of trafficking is not possible again.

Walking through the Door of No Return, I could feel the spirit of humiliation. I thought about all the things that our ancestors had endured up to that point. The efforts to break their spirits were so intense that, by the time they walked through that gate, their spirits were likely broken. And that's the irony. Our ancestors likely wept as they were traveling through that gate, but as we walked through it, maybe somewhere in the spirit world, they were rejoicing at our return.

Toni Morrison talks about the practice of remembering, and perhaps the ancestors rejoice, not just because you have historic firsts like Kamala Harris who's made it a priority to return to the continent and use her bully pulpit in this way but also because we remember. They rejoice because we honor the humiliation, the torture, and the horror they endured. They rejoice because their pain was not in vain. I don't think we talk enough about the humiliation of slavery, and that humiliation started before they walked through the Door of No Return. Their heads likely hung low as they walked through that door. And considering all that our people have been through over the course of hundreds of years, there is reason today for us to walk with our heads held high. And so was I thinking about that irony—that what was intended to break the spirit of Black people has become a source of resilience for generations when we remember the truth of who we are.

Today, visitors who pass through the Door of No Return emerge onto a beach teeming with activity. Watercraft, vendors, and children work and play in the shadow of the cannons that remain just over the castle's walls. Seeing that juxtaposition was both ironic and a little jarring for me. Slave ships that once frequented that beach have been replaced with colorful canoes and bustling fishing communities. The sands that our enslaved ancestors were forced to walk through with their ankles and wrists in shackles are now freely visited by people from across the African diaspora. The joy and pain that coexist in that space is a testament to the resilience of Africa.

GOING ALONE

A lot of questions buzzed around among the press corps. We didn't know if the vice president was going into the slave dungeons or if she would allow a reporter to follow her inside. Ultimately, none of us was allowed to accompany her. She took a couple secret service agents and her husband along with one still photographer who was allowed to go with her into one of the dungeons.

Once she emerged, the vice president walked past the row of canons that had once been used to protect Cape Coast Castle from enemy nations. She stood at the podium with the ocean in the background. Watching the waves crashing on the shore, I couldn't help thinking about the

Emotional Vice President Harris Delivering Remarks at Cape Coast Castle

number of African bodies entombed in the ocean floor. She was visibly emotional, starting her remarks, searching for the composure to continue.

"So, being here was—was immensely powerful and moving, when we think about how human beings were treated by the hundreds of thousands in this very place that we now stand, the crimes that happened here, the blood that was shed here.

"There are dungeons here where human beings were kept—men, women, and children. They were kidnapped from their homes. They were transported hundreds of miles from their homes, not really sure where they were headed. And they came to this place of horror—some to die, many to starve and be tortured, women to be raped—before they were then forcibly taken on a journey thousands of miles from their home to be sold by so-called merchants and taken to the Americas, to the Caribbean to be an enslaved people.

"We don't know the numbers who died on their way to this place, the numbers who were killed during that passage on the Atlantic. The horror of what happened here must always be remembered. It cannot be denied. It must be taught. History must be learned.

"And we must then be guided by what we know also to be the history of those who survived in the Americas, in the Caribbean—those who proudly declare themselves to be the diaspora who then came out of—in, often, many situations— odds that were designed to break them, to demoralize them, to create systems and situations that were to make them feel like less than humans, less than full human beings.

"But yet, they survived. And they tell another history—a history of endurance, a history of faith, a history in believing what is possible, a history not only that tells about the ability that each individual has to survive, but to thrive.

"And so, all these stories must be told. All these stories must be told in a way that we take from this place— the pain we all feel, the anguish that reeks from this place. And we then carry the knowledge that we have gained here toward the work that we do in lifting up all people, in recognizing the struggles of all people, of fighting for, as the walls of this place talk about, justice and freedom for all people, human rights for all people.

So, that's what I take from being here. The descendants of the people who walked through that door were strong people, proud people, people of deep faith; people who loved their families, their traditions, their culture, and carried that innate being with them through all of these periods; went on to fight for civil rights, fight for justice in the United States of America and around the world.

"And all of us, regardless of your background, have benefited from their struggle and their fight for freedom and for justice."[6]

Her remarks were maybe five or six minutes—no more than that—but in those few moments, she affirmed why we must teach this history. Listening to Vice President Harris speak about the crimes and horror that had taken place in that fortress, I felt as though her experience walking through the dungeon had been similar to mine. Her words connected the perversion of slavery with the misrepresentation of history that we are witnessing today across the United States. It felt like she was speaking to the entire diaspora, standing in her power as a Black woman and a world leader. It was an incredible moment that I fully expected to be celebrated back at home. So, I was completely shocked, disappointed, and gob-smacked when I later discovered that the viral moment trending on social media from the vice president's trip to this vital piece of Black history was a conversation around her hair snapping back to its kinky state. Even in the era of the CROWN Act, the viral social media moment was a discussion about "her kitchen" getting a little rough in the extreme heat of Ghana's Cape Coast region—not the humanity that Vice President Harris brought to a place that tried to strip us of our humanity.[7]

She was at Cape Coast Castle at a time when it felt like book bans and the movement against Black history in schools was at an apex. The vice president's remarks came in the midst of an uproar over Florida's Republican governor Ron DeSantis's decision to block a new high school advanced placement course on Black history. But instead of uplifting the Black history being made by Vice President Harris in Africa, I noticed evidence that Black Twitter chose to focus on Kamala's hair with a comical look at the battle between her blowout and the African sun.

While I understand that public figures are often the center of our jokes and commentary, the problem lies in the fact that far too many members of our community get their information about the vice president only from social media, especially our younger generations. They are not tuning into

traditional news outlets at the same rate as older generations. Most of them get their information from provocative
headlines and the misguided commentary of self-appointed
experts. As a result, a lot of bad behavior and incomplete
analysis get rewarded with undeserved likes, views, and
engagement. Our young people are extremely vulnerable to
the misinformation and disinformation campaigns that go
unregulated on social media. This is why we can't allow a
conversation about the vice president's hair to become the
overriding narrative of her trip to Ghana. People with great
influence are trying to ban our history, and we must stop
fueling their fire.

The Kamala I saw at Cape Coast Castle was visibly
moved and not in the performative way that so many politicians address the rawness of our history but in a genu-
inely human way. She does not typically wear her heart on
her sleeve, but she visibly fought back tears as she delivered
her remarks. We rarely experience her in that way, but what
I witnessed that day was a powerful woman leader standing
in her power and meeting the moment.

PROXIMITY TO BLACKNESS

There is no denying the connection between whiteness and
power across the globe. As Europeans colonized countries
around the world, they used racial categories to not only
differentiate themselves from people of darker complexions,
but they also created racial categories to separate Black

people according to the level of melanin in their skin and the straightness of their hair. This proximity to whiteness has long determined the degree of access given to Black individuals when it comes to power, resources, and social status. Lighter skin tones have historically been granted a greater level of privilege based on their proximity to whiteness while darker skinned people have been denied access to economic-building resources.

Within the Black community, proximity to whiteness has shown up as colorism. Many of us have taken these destructive mindsets as our own, using them as license to discriminate against one another based on skin color. But over the decades, as access to power has extended and the definition of Blackness has evolved, skin color has become one of many factors that Black people use when labeling someone as "kinfolk" or "skinfolk." We have turned the proximity to whiteness on its head by using proximity to Blackness as our guiding compass.

The Washington Post has published at least two pieces questioning whether Vice President Harris is Black enough.[8,9] If this conversation is taking place in the late-to-the-party mainstream media, it's a reasonable bet that it is a pervasive question among Black folks.

During her presidential campaign, Harris responded to criticisms around her Blackness in an interview with *The Breakfast Club* radio show. "I was born in Oakland," she said with a knowing laugh, "and raised in the United States, except for the years that I was in high school in Montreal, Canada. This is the same thing they did to Barack. This is not new to us. And so I think that we know what they are trying to do. They are trying to do what has been happening over the last two years, which is powerful voices trying to sow hate and division among us. And so we need to recognize when we're being played."[10]

Her point about former president Barack Obama is a valid one. We cannot ignore the fact that some of his detractors were of a darker complexion. Discussions about whether he was Black enough were taking place in barbershops across the country. But President Obama had a proximity to Blackness that many Black people valued. In 2008, even if they were unsure about Barack Obama, they were sure about Michelle. I will never forget one of my best friends telling me back then that she voted for Michelle and not Barack. For the vice president, her husband, Doug Emhoff, is clearly her person, and I saw glimpses of their adoration for one another during the trip. Yet, as likable as I found him, I don't think, for a second, he has been able to help her in the same way that Barack was helped by Michelle.

The vice president's marriage represents a departure from convention in a couple of different ways, and some people want to punish her for that. In an interracial marriage, she is stepmother to his two white children, who call her "Momala." While this is clearly a term of endearment between Harris and her blended family, it's also a source of discomfort for many, invoking the stereotype of the mammy. This discomfort was reawakened for viewers like me when daytime talk show host Drew Barrymore told Harris during an interview, "We need you to be Momala of the country."

I've since observed and participated in several conversations about this teachable moment. *The New York Times* columnist Charles Blow put it best in his "Kamala Harris Isn't Americans' 'Momala.' She's Our Vice President" op-ed when he wrote "That she would be called upon to comfort and nurture the country, rather than dutifully represent it, is demeaning and holds Black women captive to historical mythologies."[11] Blow goes on in the piece to write "It's an illustration of the nanny-fication of Black women that casts them as racialized human security blankets—forgiving, tranquil and even magical." Another area that can sometimes cause folks to reexamine one's Black card is interracial marriages of which there are several in my own family.

The number of individuals marrying people of different racial or ethnic groups has steadily increased. According to a 2021 Pew Research Center report, at least 19 percent of new marriages in the US involves spouses from different ethnic or racial groups, representing an increase from 11 percent in 2000.[12] The vice president's marriage also represents a departure from convention in terms of traditional male and female roles. He's the first Second Gentleman of the United States. The title alone is a constant reminder of who has more power outwardly. But is that any different from Oprah and Stedman whom we embrace with open arms? I called my daily radio show and podcast *A More Perfect Union* because we have to become a more perfect union from the inside out. It's not going to look the same for all of us. But what can we learn from each other?

PROXIMITY TO PAIN

The *Oxford English Dictionary* defines "unconventional" as "not following what is done or considered normal or acceptable by most people." Vice President Harris has undoubtedly lived an unconventional life. From her diverse ancestry to every step of her professional journey as a career prosecutor, she has consistently gone against the grain, refusing to follow the formula of what's considered normal by most people of color. But the reality of being an unconventional vice president has not won her the respect and loyalty of the political establishment. It also has not won her the loyalty of standard-bearers.

Terrance Woodbury is the co-founder and CEO of HIT Strategies, a public opinion research firm. Recognized as one of America's foremost pollsters and political strategists, he granted me an interview where he offered some insight on the disconnect between the vice president's unconventional life and the way she is seen by voters in our community. "We've done a lot of research with organizations like Higher Heights and Black Women's Roundtable to understand how Black women candidates are perceived by society. We found that what makes Black women more appealing as candidates is a bit of a contradiction in the way that Black women show up in politics. We've seen that what makes Black women most appealing to society is their proximity to pain. It is this idea that because of their proximity to pain, they are more empathetic to other people's pain. They are more empathetic to the needs and the pain of communities that they may not share an identity with. So, you will see the LGBTQ+ community or immigrant community or disabled communities more apt to empathize and support women of color as candidates because of that proximity to pain or that expected proximity to pain. The contradiction comes in because Black women often do the exact opposite. Instead of portraying that pain when they run, they over credential themselves—leading with all of their qualifications, degrees, and professional accomplishments."[13]

Woodbury said that Keisha Lance Bottoms exemplified a prime example of this contradiction when she ran for mayor of Atlanta. "She started introducing herself as a superior court judge, as the president of The Links, as a board member of her alma mater, Florida Agricultural and Mechanical University, better known as FAMU. When I started doing focus groups with voters, specifically young voters of color, they didn't relate with any of her professional service and accomplishments. What they did pull out of her bio was buried all the way down at the bottom of her bio, which was her father Major Lance. He went to jail, and when he was incarcerated, Kesha had to go sweep hair in her mother's hair salon to pay her way through law school."[14]

Woodbury said Bottoms's pain made her more appealing to voters than her accomplishments, a dynamic similar to what we see with Vice President Harris. "I don't think we see enough of the vice president's pain. I don't think voters are aware and acclimated and familiar and intimate with Kamala Harris's pain because she has been the first in every role that she has ever been in. She has had to lead with credentials and qualifications, and that's prevented us, as voters, from seeing the thing that would make her the most endearing."

White supremacy is not just a distraction. It is also a painful experience that continues to inflict lasting trauma, making our proximity to pain omnipresent and driving the desire of many Black voters to see vulnerability in Black female leaders, including Kamala. They are expected to share their own wounds while also being the balm to soothe the wounds of others, and when that is not done to their level of satisfaction, these voters begin to question these leaders' proximity to Blackness. Kamala's unconventional life may not look like the soothing balm to our wounds, but that does not negate her commitment to dismantling the perversion of white supremacy that causes them.

CHAPTER SIX

MY DEAR SISTER

On our last day in Ghana, the vice president held a roundtable with the press corps before we all boarded the plane to Tanzania. After a six-hour flight, we landed at approximately eleven o'clock at night local time. Though it was late, there was still a crowd of people waiting to greet the vice president and welcome her to the country. Some waved American flags along with the Tanzanian flag. And some wore T-shirts adorned with the vice president's image. She disembarked from the plane and received a bouquet of flowers before walking down a red carpet to the car that awaited her.

The next morning, a palpable excitement filled the air as we made our way to the joint press conference of Vice President Harris and Tanzanian president Samia Suluhu Hassan. Heading to the State House, I looked around at the many young women proudly displaying pictures of both women on their clothing. It reminded me of the excitement I felt at seeing Nelson Mandela speak decades before.

It dawned on me that, though her story is vastly different from that of Nelson Mandela's, the vice president being there might have meant as much to those girls in Tanzania as Nelson Mandela's visit to the Oakland Coliseum meant to me.

Seeing the Tanzanian president and the US vice president stand behind their respective podiums in front of the Tanzanian and American flags, I was struck by the significance of this historical moment. Rarely do we see two Black women standing together as world leaders. President Hassan began her remarks by recognizing the presentation of two female leaders as a historic milestone.[1] "And to put a shirt on top of all this, the meeting takes place during this very important month, Women's History Month," she said. "What an inspiration and a testimony to Tanzanian young girls. I truly thank you, Madam Vice President, for honoring my invitation and coming to visit me."[2]

After playfully asking Vice President Harris about her knowledge of a few Swahili words, President Hassan expressed her appreciation for US support in various areas of good governance and democracy. She also spoke about the US project on Respect the Ocean, which was launched by Second Gentleman Doug Emhoff. "We particularly welcome cooperation in the following areas: fishing, especially deep-sea fishing; aquafarming; salt mining; gas exploration; blue tourism; and marine transportation," she said. "These are the potential areas of investments in Tanzania with a blue economy."[3]

Tanzania has navigated a complex path in its progress towards democracy since gaining its independence in 1961. In 2020, John Magufuli, with Hassan as his running mate, campaigned to become the president of Tanzania. Though he secured more than 80 percent of the votes and was ultimately declared the winner, allegations of electoral fraud were brought from opposition parties.[4] Don't these parallels already sound eerily familiar to the US 2020 presidential election? When President Magufuli lost his life to illness in 2021, Hassan was sworn in as the nation's first woman president.

During her remarks, Vice President Harris encouraged Tanzania's movement towards maintaining a more inclusive government. "Madam President, under your leadership, Tanzania has taken important and meaningful steps. And President Joe Biden and I applaud you," she said. "You have been open to working with the political opposition. We have discussed that. You have lifted the ban on political party public rallies. You worked to improve the freedom of the press. And just yesterday, you participated, as you mentioned, in the Summit for Democracy."[5] She called President Hassan a champion of democratic reforms and credited her accomplishments with helping to expand the US partnership with Tanzania.

The vice president went on to announce a few initiatives, including the Export-Import Bank, which will facilitate up to $500 million in US exports to Tanzania, and a partnership on 5G technology and cybersecurity. Reiterating her commitment to economic development on the continent, the vice president remarked, "As I have been making clear on this trip to the continent, I believe that the innovation and ingenuity that is taking place here on the continent will shape the future of the world and will benefit the world."[6]

Charles Stith, former US ambassador to Tanzania, called the vice president's visit significant. In an interview with me, he said, "It is not the same as having the president. Nobody's confused about that. But given that Tanzania has a woman president and Kamala Harris is an African American woman and obviously the first African American woman vice president, people understood the historic nature of her visit. And after the Trump years, having someone of her rank come was important."[7] He said that after President Biden's participation in the 2022 African Leadership Summit, there were legitimate questions around whether he was just there for show. "And so having Vice President Harris show up on the continent so soon after the summit caused many people to pause and say, 'Okay, this might be really serious.' And then when you add that all of this happened before the halfway mark of [Biden's] first administration, which was also something different relative to when past presidents have visited, it did a lot for [America's] credibility on the continent."[8]

A TRANSCENDING MOMENT

One moment of the press conference left a lasting impression on me. At the start of her statements, President Hassan turned to Vice President Harris and referred to her as "my dear sister." I have no idea whether anyone else in the room recognized that remarkable moment, but for me, the unapologetic tenderness of her words transcended the moment. It was a rare glimpse into a softness that Black women of power are often denied.

Oftentimes, women leaders are critiqued for not being soft enough or tender enough. Think back to Margaret Thatcher, Hillary Clinton, and even Barbara Jordan. A recurring critique of a lot of women in power is that they have to leave behind their feminism to get that power. Now, here I was in 2023, the year of our Lord, and I am watching the president of Tanzania look over at the vice president of the United States and unapologetically refer to her in such a sweet and tender way. With the many tropes that exist about Black women, this was an important observation. Most people don't think of the word tenderness when it comes to Vice President Harris or many other Black women in power. So, it was strange that this element of the press conference didn't get more attention stateside because, depending on what side of the political aisle you're on, these two powerful Black women standing on a world stage may represent a doomsday scenario, or it may be a demonstration of a political future within the realm of possibility. However, the ascent of the current Tanzanian president serves as a reminder that anything can happen to any of us, and that exponentially increases as we get older.

President Hassan's predecessor lost his life to illness, and a Black woman of power stepped in. Then, that Black woman invited another Black woman to her country so they could both create a historical moment and provide a peek into the potential for world leadership.

WHITE GAZE AND MISOGYNOIR

Toni Morrison described the concept of the white gaze as "The little white man that sits on your shoulder and checks out everything you do or say." While she was talking about the challenge of Black writers to create a tone that doesn't center a white audience, it is my opinion that this concept has far greater reach beyond the literary world.

There is a surround sound effect that is projecting a very narrow narrative about Vice President Harris. Members of the media use the phrase "word salad" to mock her off-the-cuff remarks, staff turnovers have been used to portray her administration as filled with dysfunction, and her credentials to stand on the world stage are repeatedly brought into question. Now, I am not saying that every narrative about the vice president is 100 percent false, but I am saying that they are often extremely narrow. And for people who come from marginalized groups, who haven't had the benefit of generational power, this is a reality of a narrative driven by the white gaze with which we all must contend.

When I say in some ways, we are Kamala and Kamala is us, part of what makes her different from every former US vice president is that she's been a perpetual outsider. Even as a student at Howard University, she was a mixed Black

Indian girl at an HBCU. And I suspect that is not the dominant heritage among Black folks at any HBCU, let alone Howard. Perpetual outsider. She graduated from a public law school and decided to be a career prosecutor, to go inside to change the system from the inside out. That's not a popular career track for Black women. Perpetual outsider. Kamala Harris had the courage to run for attorney general in California and become the first Black woman to do so. Perpetual outsider. Then she had even more courage to run for the US Senate in California, becoming only the second Black woman in history to serve in the United States Senate. Say it with me—perpetual outsider. And above all, she had the audacity to make a run for president and ultimately become the first female, first Black, and first Asian-American US vice president. Now, here she is again as the perpetual outsider.

There has never been anyone like her to serve in this capacity, and the analysis around what she's doing and how well she's doing it lacks that very important piece. The people who are analyzing her are often perpetual insiders with generations of power and influence behind them. And every chance that some of the institutionalists have to stick it to her, they do. No, she doesn't walk on water, and yes, she makes mistakes. What politician doesn't? But are we asking ourselves, in our analysis of her, what is driving this super narrow narrative? And as Black folks, why are we okay with that?

In June of 2021, when she stood on that podium in Guadalajara and told would-be migrants, "Do not come," that wasn't her finest vice-presidential moment, especially as the child of immigrants, but it was also far from her only moment. I remember the buzz around then vice president Biden when he got ahead of President Obama in his support for same-sex marriage. During one of his many occasions of going off-script without White House approval, he publicly declared his comfort with same-sex married couples having identical rights as heterosexual married couples. The newspapers were filled with headlines about Vice President Biden breaking ranks with President Obama. Biden ultimately apologized, but that would not be his only blunder. As a senator, a vice president, and as a presidential contender, Biden was known to be prone to gaffs, yet he was still elected president. Can you be gaff prone and still become president as a Black woman? I think not. Then, you have Trump who is basically peddling in fascism and authoritarianism. Look at how much support he consistently enjoys, even considering his countless federal and state indictments.

As the 2024 Republican presidential candidates geared up their campaigns, it became evident pretty quickly that Vice President Harris was in their sights. Florida governor Ron DeSantis and UN ambassador Nikki Haley referred to the current administration as the Harris administration instead of the Biden-Harris administration, trying to plant seeds of fear and doubt around a potential Harris presidency. And I think this is an important moment for people who are supporters of Kamala Harris, for people who are skeptics of Kamala Harris, for people who shrug their shoulders when asked questions about Kamala Harris. I think it's an important moment for folks to ask themselves if she didn't have the potential to do the job and deliver, why would they bank their election strategy on mounting a fight against her?

This narrative of the vice president is a masterclass in misogynoir, demonstrating the confluence of gender and race-based discrimination. We saw it at the very start of her presidential campaign with folks on the Right questioning her constitutional eligibility, as a person born in the United States to immigrants, to serve as president. Then the rumblings began with those tired claims that she slept her way into positions of power. As reported by *The Washington Post*, within the first week of the vice president being named to the Biden-Harris ticket, the disgusting hashtag #heelsupharris appeared 35,479 times in Twitter posts, and false claims about the future vice president were being shared at a rate of 3,000 times an hour on Twitter.

There's potentially no more powerful signal of anti-Blackness in our government than the campaigns launched against the Harris vice presidential administration. Her mere existence in the office is at odds with white supremacy ideology at its core.

FAMILY BUSINESS

The conversations about Vice President Harris in the Black community come from different segments of Black people. I think there are some Black folks who see her as a Whitley Gilbert character as vice president. On the fictional HBCU campus of Hillman College, *A Different World*—a classic sitcom that exposed us to something we had never seen on television or thought we needed to see on television—Whitley Gilbert gave us the possibility of what going to college could look like as Black people who checked for other Black people and were unapologetic about who we were. Some Black folks take pride in Vice President Harris being a Bison and a member of Alpha Kappa Alpha Sorority. Other Black folks have no connection to or understanding of what that means, so their experiences shape their perspectives on Vice President Harris in a very different way.

I think there are Black folks across the board who are uncomfortable with her political origin story as a prosecutor. And the idea of her climbing up the political ladder, having had some hand in putting more Black men in jail, no matter how exaggerated that story may be or what parts of that story may be untrue, that is a very powerful narrative. For these folks, her credentials as a former prosecutor make her somebody who's no friend of Black people. That, in part, stems from the view of prosecutors we see on the TV where they are most often white. The perception is that they are not using their prosecutorial authority to help us. So, the fact that she made the decision to go work as a career prosecutor, for some Black folks, that's dead on arrival.

But it is my hope that the perception is being helped a little bit by the presence of other Black folks practicing law. At this moment in history, it's interesting how we are seeing Black law enforcement folks in positions of power, influence, and authority that we haven't seen before. New York

Attorney General Letitia James, a Black woman, has won a $454-million civil fraud penalty, exposing former president Trump to financial peril. Fulton County District Attorney Fani Willis, a Black woman, holding Trump accountable for alleged election interference in Georgia. Then, you have Alvin Braggs, the Manhattan district attorney who won a thirty-four-count conviction of former president Trump for falsifying New York business records in order to conceal his illegal scheme to corrupt the 2016 presidential election. It's very interesting that the very same law and order identity, political identity that Black folks have traditionally been suspicious of, and in many cases, rightfully so, has come full circle to this moment. We are seeing folks on the inside who look like us and who purport to love our community, bringing that same energy to holding the powerful accountable and making clear for the world that not even a former president is above the law. So maybe the law and order stuff is not as radioactive politically as it once was, and maybe there might be some redemption for Vice President Harris in this moment. So, if you're rooting for Letitia James but rooting against Kamala Harris, let's interrogate that. If you're rooting for Fani Willis but you're rooting against Kamala Harris, let's interrogate that. If you're rooting for Alvin Braggs's historic conviction but you're rooting against Kamala Harris, let's examine that, too.

As a person who grew up in the San Francisco Bay Area, I have been familiar with Vice President Harris since the start of her political career. Like many others, I saw promise in her as she ascended as an elected leader, but there was also a cautious optimism, largely based on her history as a prosecutor. When she announced her run for president, like many folks looking for fresh voices and new leaders, it was refreshing to witness. There were so many things about her that I could relate to as somebody who also came from an immigrant family, someone who had a consciousness around civil and human rights and fighting for social justice, somebody who was unafraid to take an unconventional path to create change. She made a decision to become a prosecutor, and she was willing to take the unpopular approach to law enforcement that wildly differed from a lot of the old white prosecutors, which is the majority of prosecutors in the state of California and across the country. She was willing to reject this imagined contrast between being tough on crime or soft on crime to try and carve out a space of asking what it could mean to be smart on crime.

Her rise was imperfect, and I can absolutely agree that her prosecutorial record should be examined and critiqued. But I also need the critics within our Black communities to acknowledge a very important point about law enforcement. The job of a district attorney, an attorney general, is to enforce the law. Yes, there is some prosecutorial discretion, but the entire job isn't prosecutorial discretion. And that's a nuance that not everybody understands or cares to understand. Similarly, in her role now as vice president, I think there are people who may make assumptions that she has more discretion than she actually does.

When then senator Harris announced her presidential campaign, I was optimistic about her potential to bring forth a different conversation in the campaign. Would she ultimately get the nomination and become president? I knew it was unlikely. But I felt excited about the potential for her to usher in a shift in terms of how we talk about politics and advance an agenda that is relevant to the lives of perpetual outsiders—people who are in the communities that I'm a part of, people who are like her and the communities that she's a part of. Honestly, up until that point, the best we could hope for was sending a really good ally to the White House—an ally to Black people, an ally to LGTBQ+ people, and an ally to protect and defend the rights of women.

With Kamala, it felt like we had a new opportunity, a very special opportunity to send somebody to the White House who was of these communities. We didn't have to take out our rubric and figure out whether or not so-and-so was a credible enough ally for us to bargain with. That was the seed of my optimism. Instead of sending the ally to do the job, we could potentially send someone who is in community to do the job, to advance the work and the agenda. So many of us are still hungry for that, which is why we say representation matters.

Let's take that a step farther. Representation matters, but there's a distinct difference between folks who are representative and folks who have a level of immersion in community. I will never forget a conversation I had years ago with Dr. Karenga, the founder of Kwanzaa, where he shared with me his operational definition of Black. What does he mean when he talks about Black folk? And one of the things he said to me was Black is color, consciousness, and commitment. This is where the hashtag movements around representation fall short. It stops at color or whatever the distinct characteristic is of said person and doesn't zero-in enough on consciousness or commitment.

For folks who have a question mark around the vice president's Black card, I would venture to say that they may suspect that she doesn't have all three of those things—maybe one or two, but not all three. But as someone who had a front row seat to this historical trip to Africa, I saw a level of consciousness and commitment that folks here at home either don't see at all, don't see enough, or aren't paying attention to consistently.

If you've ever been a first and only, a first or only, then you understand that game in your own head. You may wonder, why am I really here? Am I here for my color? Am I here for my consciousness? Am I here for my commitment? All of that? None of that? And in some rooms, you may be there because of your color, but the folks may remember that you were there in that room because of your consciousness and commitment. I think we have an opportunity to get clear about the kind of consciousness and commitment we're willing to reward with our time, with our talent, with our treasure, with our vote.

Personally, I get how some people will take a quick look and will make snap judgments about who you are and what you care about. For me, it's questions around who I am checking for as somebody who is Black and gay and first generation American-born. On my father's side, there are rooms that I go into where some people actually wonder whether I am showing up in that room as Black first. It is what Pauli Murray referred to as indivisibility, while folks like Derek Bell and Kimberly Crenshaw gave us language around intersectionality. There is not a point where my Blackness ends and my queerness begins or where my compassion, my empathy, my immersion in immigrant communities begins or ends. And I think there's a real opportunity for us as we become more of a multicultural nation, where people who formerly sat on the periphery of power now sit in the seats of power. As they take their seats, we must re-examine how and why we are standing in the way.

Kamala's very existence challenges the assumptions of some people. She is the first Black, first Indian, and first woman US vice president. The idea that those things can coexist makes people uncomfortable. A Maxine Waters type vice president would be a lot more palatable for them. They understand that school of Blackness. She's affectionately referred to as Auntie Maxine for a reason. She gets auntie status because we know her, and she knows us—full stop. Kamala may not feel like a clean win because we share her as a historic first on so many different fronts. That disrupts some people's thinking because they don't feel that they can just root for her as a Black person or simply as a woman. At her best, Kamala represents a generational shift in terms of her path to power, her relationship with the establishment, and her willingness to disrupt the status quo with a level-headed political pragamatism. She is not an Auntie Maxine, and that's okay. Black people are not a monolith, so why are we willing to put limitations on the possibility model Kamala offers as a Black leader?

Kamala often talks about the concept of being unburdened by what has been and motivated by what can be.

Think about other history-making political leaders like Shirley Chisolm. Her big claim to fame was being the first Black woman elected to Congress and the first Black woman to run for president. Though she did not win the party nomination, her candidacy and advocacy represented a possibility model. The win was changing hearts and minds around what was possible for women and, particularly, Black women. Sometimes, we minimize the lasting impact that these leaders may have on the political landscape because we work from the narrow definition of a win. But for Black folks across the diaspora, winning isn't necessarily being the victor on election. It is also shaping what is possible on the day after the election and beyond.

I remember being a student at University of Southern California during the 2004 election cycle, and Rev. Al Sharpton was among the candidates who came to campus for a Democratic presidential debate. I don't think most people believed that he was going to capture the Democratic nomination and be elected president, but that experience taught me that he played an incredibly important role as an activist candidate. He made sure that issues of importance to the Black community were put front and center in the conversations on the debate stage and campaign trail. In the spirit of activist presidential candidates like Shirley Chisolm, Jesse Jackson, and Rev. Al Sharpton, the political profile of Vice President Harris and the Africa trip exemplify the redefinition of winning. She showed us what can happen when

Black leaders use their platforms to spotlight and illuminate possibilities that we may not otherwise see. However, illuminating what's possible and making a material difference in the lives of Black folks an ocean apart are not one in the same.

CHAPTER SEVEN

DIGITAL INCLUSION

A concerning contrast exists across the continent of Africa where the promise of a digital future clashes with the harsh realities of digital exclusion. The creative genius and bustling tech innovations give a glimpse of the unlimited amount of potential. Within large cities, smartphones abound, and young entrepreneurs navigate online commerce, seizing opportunities in the global marketplace. Yet, just beyond the city limits, a different story unfolds due to limited infrastructure and sparse connectivity. Remote villages struggle to connect with the outside world, essentially silencing their voices. In these forgotten corners of Africa, the consequences of digital exclusion are profound. Without access to online resources, healthcare remains a distant hope for many.

Even in 2024, entire segments of the population remain isolated from the digital age. Young minds are limited to the information they find in outdated textbooks, talented entrepreneurs are limited to the economic opportunities of their surroundings. And the simple digital advantages that so many of us take for granted every day are a distant dream. Across the continent, the digital divide casts a shadow over their aspirations for a brighter future.

Vice President Harris highlighted this issue on the final day of her trip across Western Africa saying, "There are many areas of focus of this public-private partnership, but there are some in particular that I believe have been most effective and are the main focus of my trip this time. And one of them is the issue of digital inclusion."[1]

She spoke about the importance of digital services to twenty-first century economies and their ability to create broad opportunities. "Digital technologies facilitate opportunities across society and, frankly, I believe can be great equalizers in terms of giving those who have access equal opportunity and availability to information, to education, to networks in a way that improves and empowers themselves, their families, their community, and all of society benefits. And, of course, when we talk about digital access, we are talking about everything from financial inclusion to economic opportunities, all of which obviously drive growth and innovation. Africa's digital economy is large and growing. Within the next two years, for example, the forecast is that one in six of the world's [i]nternet users will be right here on this continent. One in six."[2]

Vice President Harris went on to showcase some African countries where digital solutions are creating economic opportunities. She mentioned Kenya's mobile phone payment systems, the fintech innovations happening in Nigeria, and health products that are being delivered by drones in some areas of Ghana. "Yet, in other places on the continent, we see that there is a lag and that there are many who lag behind," she said. "And we must be clear about the challenges presented to close these gaps and then commit to take action, because solutions are within sight and within reach."[3]

The Digital Divide

According to a United Nations Office to the African Union 2022 policy brief, "Digital inclusion in the Women, Peace and Security Agenda in Africa," only 17.8 percent of Africans have internet access in their homes, and a mere 10.7 percent have home-based computers.[4] Without access to digital tools and the internet, individuals and communities miss out on opportunities for entrepreneurship, e-commerce, and participation in the global digital economy.

Armed with talent and determination, Africa's entrepreneurs know no bounds. Yet, the lack of access to digital technologies creates a formidable enemy to success. Limited access to digital tools and the internet hinders their ability to compete in the global marketplace.

The digital divide also negatively impacts healthcare resources. In a region of the world where limited access to quality medical services creates significant healthcare challenges, digital exclusion exacerbates these issues, leaving communities underserved and vulnerable. Without access to telemedicine services, health information portals, and digital health records, patients in rural areas may deal with poorer health outcomes and unnecessary suffering. How much better would these outcomes be if patients had access to telemedicine services? What if patients could access health information portals to learn more about their symptoms and treatment options? What if medical records were stored digitally, allowing for a continuity of care regardless of location? Investment in the expansion of technology will give the people of Africa the tools to revolutionize healthcare delivery.

Limited infrastructure, such as unreliable electricity and limited internet connectivity, poses barriers to the widespread adoption of digital healthcare solutions. But technological solutions must also address the underlying socio-economic disparities and inequities that span across education programs and healthcare for all.

Digital exclusion can also exclude entire communities from full participation in governance and civic participation. In countries where political tensions run high and access to information is tightly controlled by the government, the lack of digital exclusion helps perpetuate authoritarian rule. Without access to independent news sources or social media platforms, vulnerable citizens fall prey to propaganda, eroding trust in democratic institutions. Voting processes can also be hindered, making the digital divide a threat to democracy in African countries. When individuals find themselves excluded from essential government programs and services due to an inability to access information or seek assistance when needed, they feel unheard, disconnected, and disempowered. Without access to online platforms and social media, they may also feel sidelined in the struggle for social justice and equality.

Bridging the Digital Divide

Since making her maiden voyage to the continent, Vice President Harris has not stopped working the phones to make good on the Biden-Harris Administration's commitment to the shared prosperity between the US and Africa. During the 2024 Kenya State Visit, Vice President Harris announced another round of public and private sector commitments to advance digital inclusion in Africa. According to White House officials, these commitments include the following:

- Launch of the Mobilizing Access to the Digital Economy (MADE) Alliance powered by the African Development Bank Group and Mastercard. The Alliance aims to provide digital access to critical services for 100 million individuals and businesses in Africa over the next ten years with an initial focus on supporting women and the agriculture sector. The pilot program in 20204 aims to provide digital access for three million farmers in Kenya, Tanzania, and Nigeria before quickly expanding to Uganda, Ethiopia, Ghana, and the rest of the continent.
- Launch of non-profit Partnership for Digital Access in Africa to support African institutions to double the

number of people connected to and meaningfully using the internet in Africa from 40 percent to 80 percent, connecting one billion people by 2030. The initiative also aims to increase connectivity for women and girls from 30 percent to 80 percent.

To help close the digital gender gap hampering women's economic participation and access to critical online services, Vice President Harris launched the Women in the Digital Economy Fund with initial investment of $50 million from the United States Agency for International Development and $10 million from Bill and Melinda Gates Foundation. She recently announced that the Fund and related Women in the Digital Economy Initiative have now generated over $1 billion in public and private commitments to accelerate gender digital equality for a total of $3 billion in total commitments for women's economic empowerment initiatives.

GENDER GAP

According to the White House Fact Sheet on the vice president's launch of global initiatives on the economic empowerment of women, approximately 260 million more men than women were using the internet globally in 2022.[5] The disparity is especially prevalent in countries across Africa, where International Telecommunication Union data show that 66 percent of women do not use the internet. To address these global disparities, the Biden-Harris Administration pledged to partner with other governments, the private sector, foundations, and multilateral organizations to "improve meaningful access to equitable digital finance and other online services, and address social norms that prevent women from participating fully in the digital economy."[6]

In March 2023, the same month of our trip, Vice President Harris introduced a series of investments and initiatives "to foster women's political, economic, and social inclusion in Africa, building upon initiatives launched at the U.S.-Africa Leaders Summit in December 2022, including the Digital Transformation with Africa (DTA) Initiative."[7] These programs included $60 million to launch the Women in the Digital Economy Fund with at least half focused towards Africa, nearly $400 million in private sector commitments to support closure of the gender digital divide, and $528 million in private sector commitments to support women's economic empowerment in Africa with targeted support for gender programming more broadly. Building upon the 2022 US-Africa Leaders Summit, $47 million in US government initiatives were set aside to advance gender equality across Africa.

The vice president also announced nearly $400 million in private sector and philanthropic commitments in support of the Women in the Digital Economy Fund, which includes significant contributions to the continent.[8]

At the heart of the digital gender gap in Africa lies a complex web of socio-economic, cultural, and structural barriers that inhibit women and girls' access to and use of digital technologies. In many parts of the continent, traditional gender roles and norms dictate that women are responsible for household chores and caregiving, leaving little opportunity or willingness for them to engage with technology. The consequences of disparities affect societies and economies as a whole, resulting in women being excluded from today's most significant economic opportunities. This can restrict their ability to support their families and contribute to economic growth. The lack of access to digital information and resources can also leave women in Africa vulnerable to social isolation, disempowerment, and exploitation. They may face substantial barriers to healthcare services, making the gender gap a public health issue as well. Maternal mortality rates can soar as expectant mothers lack access to vital medical services, and treatable illness can become life-threatening events.

Broad policies and regulatory reforms are needed to create an enabling environment for digital gender inclusion in Africa. Governments must prioritize investment in digital infrastructure, including expanding access to electricity and internet connectivity in rural areas, to ensure that women and girls have the necessary tools to access and use digital technologies. Moreover, efforts to promote digital literacy and skills development must be inclusive and accessible to women and girls of all backgrounds, including those with disabilities and from marginalized communities. Furthermore, governments and policymakers must enact laws and policies that promote gender equality and protect women's rights in the digital sphere. This includes addressing online harassment and violence against women, ensuring equal access to digital financial services and property rights, and promoting women's participation and leadership in the tech sector and digital economy. During her trip, Vice President Harris highlighted these challenges and the vital importance of bridging the digital gender gap in Africa.

Educational Divide

During the COVID-19 pandemic, children all over the world relied on digital resources to continue with their most basic educational skills. In the US, the urgency of the situation revealed significant gaps in digital inclusion for students living in rural households and those in lower-income families.[9] Students from affluent backgrounds enjoyed access to quiet, well-equipped learning environments, while others faced additional distractions from insecurities around their most basic needs. The pandemic disrupted traditional learning structures with the most the long-term academic impact landing on already marginalized groups.

As awful as the problems experienced in the US educational system were during that time, they pale in comparison to what students across the continent of Africa experienced. School closures exacerbated already existing educational inequalities, and those inequities continue today. According to a UNESCO report, 89 percent of learners across Sub-Saharan Africa still do not have access to household computers, and 82 percent lack internet access.[10] Without access to online learning resources, educational apps, and digital libraries, the skills and education that students need for future employment and economic advancement remain out of reach, perpetuating cycles of poverty and inequality. Schools struggle to provide even the most basic educational resources, let alone access to the internet or digital learning platforms. For students who call these communities home, the digital divide is a harsh reality that threatens to derail their educational aspirations.

Limited access exacerbates digital gender disparities at a young age, as girls are less likely than boys to attend school and receive training in digital skills. According to UNESCO, in sub-Saharan Africa, nine million girls between the ages of six and eleven will never attend school, compared to six million boys. This gap hampers women's ability to participate in the digital economy but also perpetuates cycles of poverty and marginalization.

But even in areas where schools can provide internet access, students still face a deficit from lack of access in their homes. It creates a problem that educators refer to as a homework gap where the lack of educational resources in the home leaves school-aged children without the ability to complete homework assignments or access learning materials outside of school.[11]

DIGITAL INVESTMENT

Vice President Harris wrapped up her digital divide remarks by speaking about the opportunities that exist with greater inclusivity. "So, this last point is such a big one in terms of what—when people are connected to the [i]nternet, when they are digitally connected, what it does in terms of opening up information sources and opportunities and access that are unimaginable without it.

"I believe it is particularly important, again, that we focus on inclusion of women and youth. And I call on representatives of the private sector to collaborate with each other, as you do already, and with our administration so we can identify synergies and support each other's work. And I would like just for a moment for us to think about the enormous possibilities that exist for growth and the use of technology—if, for example, as I described, a farmer can prepare for extreme weather or find new markets for their crops; a female entrepreneur can sell her goods through an online retailer; young people can take classes online; elderly people can have access to telehealth—and all that that will do to improve the quality of their life. By advancing digital inclusion, I believe we will be able to drive development in all of these mentioned sectors and so many more."[12]

In my interview with Color of Change's Rashad Robinson, he spoke about the potential impact of artificial intelligence (AI) technology on the continent. He said that while his hope lies in the brilliance, creativity, and innovation of the African people, his concern stems from the potential of corporations to use these opportunities as another way to carve up the continent. "There is not even an iota of trust that we can have in corporate America to do what is right on the continent of Africa. If we really are focused on making sure that AI can be of benefit, then we need rules. We need accountability. And then we need actual consequences when those rules are broken. Part of what happens in these technology spaces is that we're supposed to accept that the people behind it are going to be altruistic inside of capitalist structures when, in fact, that's just not how things work.

"We can go back to when people began talking about social media. Arab Spring opened up all of these like spaces and opportunities, but we didn't get any rules around it. It was going to just help more people come together, but then what happened? I wake up this morning to Elon Musk, tweeting about illegal immigrants—his words not mine—ruining our country. I wake up to algorithms that are feeding and amplifying that narrative. I wake up to stories about how AI is being used in political ads to distort Donald Trump's relationship with Black voters and Black people. I wake up to all these things that are like kerosene on a match. That is what results when self-regulated companies are unregulated companies. These companies on the continent of Africa will be there to extract, just like their forefathers. Yes, there will be some winners here and there, but those winners will be far and few."[13]

Amid the challenges, there are glimmers of hope. Across the continent, grassroots initiatives are springing up, determined to bridge the digital gap and expand access to quality education. In countries like Ghana and Senegal, innovative projects are harnessing the power of technology to transform education and empower students. In Nairobi, innovation centers provide young Africans with the tools and equipment they need to harness the power of technology. In Rwanda, solar-powered internet kiosks are being set up in rural villages to expand connectivity into remote communities.[14]

Yet, for every success story, there are countless challenges that remain, from limited infrastructure to entrenched socio-economic disparities. Vast areas of land remain disconnected from the digital grid with inadequate telecommunications networks and sparse internet coverage leaving millions on the wrong side of the digital divide.

Infrastructure alone is not enough to overcome the entrenched socio-economic disparities that plague the continent. In many places, access to digital technologies remains a luxury reserved for the privileged few. The elevated costs of devices and data further exacerbate the divide, creating barriers that are difficult to surmount. In addition, the diversity of languages, cultures, and customs present their own set of challenges. With over 2,000 languages spoken across the continent, the lack of localized content and digital resources in indigenous languages hinders access to information for millions of people. On a continent where cultural identity and language are deeply intertwined, the absence of linguistic diversity in the digital sphere perpetuates marginalization and exclusion.

The journey to digital inclusion on the continent of Africa requires a multifaceted approach—one that addresses the root causes of inequality while also empowering communities to further their own efforts towards a more connected future. Investment in infrastructure alone is not sufficient without additional initiatives to promote digital literacy and skills development. This requires engagement with local stakeholders, including governments, civil society organizations, and grassroots initiatives, to co-create solutions that are contextually relevant and culturally sensitive.

UBUNTU

Ubuntu is an ancient Bantu philosophy that describes community as a building block of society. It represents oneness and interconnected humanity. I grew up with the philosophy of collective responsibility, and my parents never gave me the sense that Africa needed saving. Even though my dad lived here in the US, I remember him sending things back home from time to time. I remember these band uniforms from one of the local high schools that folks were getting ready to get rid of. My dad told them, "Don't get rid of those. Let me send those back to Ghana." And he did. For a number of months, we had all these Pittsburgh Pirates band uniforms in our garage, waiting until he had enough money to ship them overseas. It also wasn't uncommon for my dad to pick up books and other items to send back. That was sort of the culture in which we grew up. A lot of our old clothes and hand-me-downs would eventually be shipped back as well. But none of this was done out of a need to "save" Africa. It was done out of a profound sense of collective responsibility.

It is not just about what we are going to do to save people in Africa from famine. It's not just about what you are doing to save African people from public health disasters. It's not just about what you are doing to provide humanitarian aid. We must have a higher standard in terms of our activities in Africa. I think that was part of the vice president's message on digital inclusion. It is a necessary aspect of investing in entrepreneurship. She is saying that we are not bound to the "save the children" approach on the continent. African people don't need the US or anybody else to save them. If anything, they have been starved out of the investment that other folks have benefited from. And if you really think about it, Kamala's approach is actually kind of revolutionary for a US vice president.

African people need a devoted partner that's not motivated by competition with some third party. They need investment. Just as the US has national security interests, so do they. Just as we have challenges with governance, so do they. Just as there are human rights questions that come up here when it comes to the relationship between community and law enforcement, similar questions arise there. Just as we have political leaders who pedal in the possibilities of turning their opponents into political prisoners, so do they.

For Black Americans who feel disconnected from the continent, there is benefit in ubuntu, the recognition of those similarities and the possibilities for the future. As Dr. Maya Angelou often said, when you know better, you do better. Understanding those connections helps us to understand that we are not alone and that we have more to lose than others might suggest. When Trump first ran for the presidency, he tried to woo Black voters by asking, "Well, what do you have to lose?" If you are operating in a space where you're just thinking about your family, or your neighborhood, or your particular state—when you're not thinking globally about what's happening to Black people—you are missing a valuable piece of the assessment. And when I say, "what's happening," I'm not talking about just what's happening through a deficit lens but what's also happening through our asset lenses. There is innovation coming out of Africa, and digital inclusion can elevate those contributions beyond our dreams. Most people do not know about this aspect of the continent, and I certainly wouldn't have known about it had Kamala not taken the trip in 2023.

EXPECTATIONS EXCEEDED

I didn't know that two-thirds of the folks who have access to the internet across Africa are mostly men. That is mind blowing to me in the twenty-first century, an era where we see this competition that creates more social media platforms and more digital streaming services. For heaven's sake, we live in the era of Apple's Siri and Amazon's Alexa. I think about how much of our world is right in the palm of our hand and how much commerce moves through our smartphones. So many of us survived the darkest days of the pandemic through the palm of our hand. Whether we're talking about our banking, communicating with loved ones, ordering groceries, or purchasing supplies on Amazon or Costco, there is so much of our life that exists at our convenience. Yet, countless women across the continent don't have the opportunity to use the same tools that we have to enjoy the same quality of life. They don't have the same comforts that we have or access to some of the success in business and entrepreneurship as we have.

Women's economic empowerment and gender equity were major themes throughout the vice president's visit to Africa. In the months prior, she literally worked the phones to rally CEOs and business leaders for contributions and deliverables, while also working internally to secure economic investments from the US government. Public private partnerships were absolutely critical to the success of the trip. Her policy team met with multiple governmental agencies for months to bring the vice president's objectives to fruition, and the trip was the final push to ensure that it all got done. Simply announcing an initiative does not equate to success, even when it's announced by the vice president of the US, but the trip provided a robust exclamation point that will compel a private sector response for years to come. Speaking about the trip in a conversation with a former White House official, they expressed to me that it was clear from the joy they witnessed on Kamala's face that her expectations were met and even exceeded.

CHAPTER EIGHT

A HISTORIC INDICTMENT

A rriving in Zambia for the vice president's press confer-ence, I was struck by the huge billboards welcoming her back to the country. She and her sister, Maya, visited Lusaka in the late 1960s during a pivotal time in Zambia's history. The country was navigating its early years of independence from Britain, a takeover that began in 1888 when the British companies obtained mineral rights from local tribal chiefs. In 1911, the countries that we now refer to as Zambia and Zimbabwe were combined into one region called Northern Rhodesia, and the British took administration over it in 1923. For decades, British authorities removed copper from the rich mines of Rhodesia, and by the late 1950s, public outcry against their colonization had reached a fever pitch with Africans demanding for greater participation in gov-ernment and political control.

When the British government declared that the days of colonialism on the continent of Africa were ending, Northern Rhodesia became the Republic of Zambia, and the remaining area became Zimbabwe. While Zambia was able to find some political footing following its independence, Zimbabwe experienced political and social unrest, causing an influx of refugees into Zambia.

The maternal grandfather of Vice President Harris, P. V. Gopalan, was a senior diplomat in the Indian government, living in Zambia after its independence. The Indian government sent him to assist in the management of refugees. It was during this time that five-year-old Kamala Harris played on the rich copper soil of Lusaka.

Her brief childhood experience had quite obviously created a connection between herself and the people of Zambia. Cheers could be heard from the moment she stepped out of Air Force Two, and as she made her way down the red carpet on the tarmac, the vice president stopped to show her appreciation of the traditional Zambian dancers who celebrated her arrival.

The crowd that waited to greet her included people of all ages. Some waved small American flags, and others yelled out their love for her. Young students dressed in their school uniforms held her hands as they asked her to feel at home in their country. Stopping to speak with a group of young women who waited to greet her, the vice president said, "All of you young leaders are what I dream about. You make me so confident in the future. You dream with ambition … you don't ever have to ask anyone's permission to lead. You were born leaders." Her arrival in Zambia was a beautiful continuation of the reverence that had been shown to the vice president upon every arrival of the trip.

I AM NOT GOING TO COMMENT

The joint press conference with Zambian president Hakainde Hichilema took place outside with the beautiful nature of the country providing a perfect background complete with giraffes, zebras, and monkeys in plain view. After welcoming Vice President Kamala Harris and her delegation, President Hichilema expressed his appreciation for the strong relationship that has existed between the United States and Zambia, one that he said is "… anchored on a number of common values, beliefs: constitutionalism; rule of law; protection of human beings, our own citizens, global citizens so they can feel safe as they go about doing their normal business in their homes, in their workplaces, and elsewhere."[1]

President Hichilema went on to address the economic concerns of his country, an issue that lay at the heart of the vice president's visit. "And we know when we unlock the debt, more investments will come," he said. "We know that when more investments come, we'll create jobs for our young people. As an African country, a number of our people population is young. And we have to take care of them. Not just jobs, but business opportunities as well. So, we are keen to invest in our people skills, keen to invest in technology. To share with you your advances in technology is something that we place a premium on because it will help … equalize things."[2] The president finished his remarks by, once again, welcoming the vice president home.

Vice President Harris began her remarks by speaking about her time in Zambia as a young girl. "My grandfather

Joint Press Conference with Vice President Harris of the US
and President Hakainde Hichilema of Zambia

was a civil servant in India. And in 1966, shortly after Zambia's independence, he came to Lusaka to serve as a director of relief measures and refugees... I remember my time here fondly. I was a child, so it is the memory of a child. But I remember being here and just how it felt, and the warmth and the excitement that was present. And, in fact, I was talking with my aunt recently, and she was reminding me of the relationships that she made when she was working at—then it was called Lusaka Central Hospital—when she was working with the physicians there. So, from my family and from all of us, we extend our greetings and hello to everyone here."[3]

The vice president went on to emphasize the importance of global cooperation, acknowledging Zambia's role as a co-chair of the second Summit for Democracy. She also spoke about the country's focus on rebuilding its economy and supporting vulnerable populations. Vice President Harris proclaimed the US's commitment to assisting Zambian leaders with the creation of an environment conducive to investment and trade, also announcing new programs to promote anti-corruption efforts, governance reforms, and financial transparency within the country.

After both leaders completed their prepared remarks, the floor was opened to questions from the press corps. *The Wall Street Journal* reporter Annie Linsky asked the both of them to comment on the indictment of former US president Donald Trump, which had been announced that morning. (In case you've lost count, this was the first Trump indictment.) The press corps had already been alerted to the indictment, and we all agreed that it was important to pose the question. Vice President Harris declined to answer the question, stating "I am not going to comment on an ongoing criminal case as it relates to the former president."[4] No surprises. We knew it was unlikely that she would make a statement or answer that question in any way, let alone a robust way. But in my view, the showstopper was the response from the Zambian president.

President Hichilema took a different route by choosing to respond. But he did it in a way that took Trump out of the equation. "I think let's remove names from your question," he said. "Let's put what we decided we will do to govern ourselves in an orderly manner. First, our constitutions, bedrock law. Then, secondary laws, other regulations create a platform or framework around which we agreed, either as Americans or as Zambians, to govern ourselves. And so, to live within those confines. And when there's transgression against law, it does not matter who is involved. I think that is what the rule of law means."[5]

The Zambian president has a cadence similar to Nelson Mandela's when he speaks, and he's very easy to listen to. And, I thought he was very effective in reminding us that you have to take Trump out of it—that it's really about respect for the rule of law. His words put the US on notice that there are democracies in Africa and around the world that are paying attention to whether or not America walks the walk when it comes to that talk. Are we going to be who we say we are?

I also found President Hichilema's response extremely interesting given his political history. During his first run for president, in April 2017, while serving as the leader of Zambia's United Party for National Development, Hichilema was arrested under the orders of President Edgar Lungu, a political rival, and charged with treason after his convoy failed to give way to President Lungu's motorcade during an event. The United Party for National Development had refused to acknowledge Lungu as the legitimate winner of the 2016 elections under suspicions of corruption. In response, Lungu alleged that Hichilema was conspiring to ensure he would be afforded the status of the president of Zambia. The arrest sparked condemnation internally and internationally. Widespread protests called for his immediate release under allegations of authoritarianism of Lungu's regime. After four months in detention, Hichilema's case was finally brought to trial, but the charges were eventually withdrawn due to persistent public pressure. In 2022, he ran against Lungu, the incumbent at the time, and prevailed.

His political background gave President Hichilema a uniquely situated perspective. So, I was just shocked his response to the Trump indictment did not get much traction in the American press. I mean, he was a political prisoner who was arrested by his predecessor. And only after immense public pressure was he released. He runs for president, and he wins. This man was not speaking in the abstract. He is somebody who understands the consequences when the rule of law doesn't prevail and when presidents are able to make their opponents into political prisoners for personal gain.

President Hichilema's response was a powerful moment that was seared in my memory. So many times, I've been told that one of the most exciting parts of being a journalist is getting to write a first draft of history. This was the first time I really felt like I was in the front row of history on the international stage, instead of in the cheap seats. Leaders around the world pay attention to what we do in this country, whether it's on the local level, state level, or federal level. They're paying attention to our democratic experiment, and when we turn away from our espoused values, it diminishes our ability to hold our friends and foes overseas accountable. They say, "Why don't you handle your backyard? When you get that worked out, then you can come talk to us."

A FOUNDATION OF DEMOCRACY

During our interview, NAACP president and CEO Derrick Johnson offered some insight on the American democratic experiment, explaining that capitalism and democracy are two separate things. "Democracy is the form of governance where individuals are able to give voice, and when it's working correctly, it can really amplify the voices of individuals to collectively determine how they prioritize public policy to create a quality of life. Capitalism is the mode of how people generate revenue. When democracy is weak and capitalism is strong, people get exploited. But when democracy is strong, it holds capitalism in check to ensure a more equitable distribution of opportunities and wealth."[6] He described American democracy as a sliding pendulum, and he said that, as that sliding pendulum continues to exist, we're going to see either "a weak democracy that's unable to hold capital in check to ensure people are not harmed and exploited or a strengthened democracy where the governance structure keeps capital in control in a way in which people could still make a lot of money and a good living, but others are not taken advantage of or exploited, and the environment is not compromised for future inhabitants."[7]

According to Johnson, the outcome of the 2024 US presidential election will have far-reaching effects across the continent of Africa. "The choice in November is not a choice between two individuals or two political parties. It's a choice of whether or not we have a functioning democracy or fascism. And if we devolve into fascism, you will see a ripple effect around the globe that will put everyone in danger. There are no guardrails in place, particularly on the continent of Africa, to keep people from being harmed by individuals and corporations that undermine established procedures and policies. [I recently read that a] rating agency determined that

Ghana is the second most safest country on the continent. That's important. But if Ghana finds itself with a governance structure that has been compromised, if people lose faith and corporations are able to exploit the country, scarcity sets in. Where you have scarcity, you have an increase in harm to individuals, to children, to those who are disadvantaged. So, we [in America] need to do all we can to try to maintain some level of foundation around democracy that we can build on because, without it, we are starting from a foundation that's beneath anything that we've seen in recent history."[8]

The conversation around democracy in African countries has become even more vital to the continent's future due to the high priority that China has placed on fostering connections in Africa. Along with diplomatic visits to the continent, the Chinese government has made significant investments in infrastructure projects across the continent, including the expansion of the Belt and Road Initiative. Primarily driven by economic motives, China seeks access to Africa's natural resources, while African nations gain the economic investment that they need to strengthen their economies as well as their global standing.

But behind the economic narrative, China is increasingly expanding its political involvement in some African nations by engaging in their political and electoral processes, promoting communist ideas, and backing political leaders who align with Chinese interests. While some African leaders have embraced support from China to further their own agendas, others have shown a democratic resilience. But the balance remains a delicate one where the overwhelming presence of

Chinese influence on the nations of Africa could have profound implications for democracy on the continent as a whole.

I interviewed Dr. Wayne A. I. Frederick, previous president of Howard University, and asked his thoughts about what is at stake in the relationship between the US and the continent of Africa. He discussed his concerns about global positioning. "I am concerned that where China has positioned itself across the world, and especially on the African continent, the US has fallen significantly behind," he said. "I just returned from Dominica, and there is a new airport being built there by the Chinese. I travel to Jamaica often. There is a road leading to the Kingston Airport that gets flooded a lot. The Chinese have gone in there and fixed that issue. In Trinidad, where I am from, they have built an amphitheater for the arts that looks very much like the Sydney Opera House. China has really put itself out in the world to ensure those relations are high."[9]

Frederick said that a conversation around this issue commanded his attention while visiting Africa as part of the US delegation. He was flipping through channels in his hotel room when he stopped to watch an interesting conversation. "I listened to a talk show where the commentator was discussing why Ghana and African countries should align themselves with China versus the US. I sat there for ninety minutes enthralled because of the nature of the conversation. It was ironic that the conversation was taking place while the vice president was there, but a lot of very salient points were being made on both sides."[10] He said he worries that America will not involve itself in that type of dialogue.

"Are we more likely to get into that conversation with VP Harris involved? I would hope so, but I think America has to get involved in that conversation, regardless of who is in that office. I think that is what's at stake. For young Africa up and coming to not have the types of relationships that China has been building is a mistake."[11]

WHAT'S AT STAKE

As people of African descent living in the US, the analysis of what's at stake can look like a web of consequential competing interests. From a global standpoint, the implications of African countries aligning more closely with China could challenge US economic interests on the continent, potentially limiting access to key resources, strategic markets, and necessary partnerships. African nations may prioritize Chinese investment and trade partnerships, resulting in reduced opportunities for American businesses to access African markets.

In my interview with Charles Stith, former US ambassador to Tanzania, he spoke about the interests of global superpowers in extracting natural resources like manganese from the continent. "The Chinese have made it clear that they want to lead the world in terms of green technologies in the battery space," he said. "And their big advantage has been that they export 90 percent of the graphite. They also control nickel and cobalt, as well as manganese."[12] Graphite, nickel, cobalt, and manganese are all essential for the manufacturing of electric vehicle batteries, so the dominance that

China asserts over the processing and/or distribution allows the country to dominate the market.[13] "With the rest of the world having to depend on them to play catch up, Africa is in the catbird seat," explained Stith, referring to efforts by the US and other Western nations to decrease their dependence on China. That's where Tanzania's graphite mining licenses enter this important conversation. These permits, granted by the Tanzanian government, allow the licensed entities to conduct mining operations in specified areas exclusively. According to geological studies, massive graphite deposits exist in the central and southeast regions of the country.[14] Tanzania also has significant deposits of manganese and is home to the largest nickel project in the world, as Stith explained. "So, if the United States and the West are going to effectively position themselves for this transition [into green energy] and continue to be epicenters economically while in the midst of this transition, they have to do business with Africa."

Global power dynamics are in play as the US navigates a world where China's influence continues to grow, but we must also ask ourselves what's at stake for the people of Africa. China's economic engagement often comes with less stringent conditions compared to Western partners, potentially undermining efforts by the United States to promote governance standards, transparency, and human rights in Africa. The presence of democratic governance tends to promote the stable and transparent environments that attract foreign investment, including from American corporations. Democracies often have more predictable legal frameworks, protection of property rights, and reduced corruption—all of which are attractive to public and private entities seeking investment opportunities on the continent.

In many ways, the ambassador's insight accentuated the vice president's strategy in distinguishing the trip as one driven by innovation and entrepreneurship. But I can't celebrate her approach without also applauding the humanitarian efforts of US leaders before her, efforts that laid the groundwork for public health stability in various parts of Africa. In 2003, US president George W. Bush launched the President's Emergency Plan for AIDS Relief (PEPFAR), investing more than $100 billion in funding for the global HIV/AIDS response.[15] The legislation has enjoyed a level of bipartisan support we rarely see anymore, spanning ten US congresses and four presidential administrations. Speaking with me about the impact of PEPFAR in our interview, Ambassador Stith said that no American president prior to Bush and, unfortunately, since Bush has done as much substantively. "The most that we were able to raise for HIV AIDS during the Clinton administration was half a billion dollars," he explained. "During Bush's first and second administration, it was $45 billion."[16]

Stith said that while PEPFAR was extremely impactful, one of the most significant initiatives undertaken by the Bush administration was the Millennium Challenge Account (MCA), which was formed to help burgeoning democracies around the world. Sound governance and policies were conditions for receipt of funding. At a ceremony announcing the program, then president Bush stated that the account was "devoted to projects in nations that govern justly, invest in their people and encourage economic freedom."[17]

"The Bush administration was spot-on when they said failed states are a breeding ground for a terrorist attack," said Stith. "We need to deal with dysfunctional states and keep them from becoming failed states." The MCA invested money into helping countries across the continent deal with crucial infrastructure needs like roads, bridges, and educational systems. Stith told me that cynics initially questioned whether any MCA grants would be awarded to African nations. "As it turned out, all of the initial grants went to African countries, and it made a huge difference across the continent," he said.[18]

Since its founding in 2004, the Millennium Challenge investments have delivered clean water to African nations and sanitation efforts to help fight disease.[19] The funds have also helped bring agricultural technologies to farmers and increased access to electricity for households and businesses. Speaking with Ambassador Stith made me realize that, without the lasting impacts of efforts like PEPFAR and the MCA, there would be no groundwork in place for Vice President Harris to focus on and champion innovation, entrepreneurship, and gender and economic justice.

A GLOBAL LEADER

As I watched the vice president wrap up the final joint press conference of the trip, in light of Trump's historic indictment back home, I thought about the dichotomy that exists between the example of a global leader that I saw standing at the podium and the loud criticisms of her international leadership abilities in the US. Her antagonists criticize her for not having a lot of formal international experience as an elected official, but standing before me was a leader whose childhood and familial exposure to the world beyond the shores of the US had strengthened her ability to exceptionally represent America on this international stage.

Errin Haines, editor-at-large of *The 19th*, was also part of the press corps that traveled to Africa with the vice president. I interviewed her on the day of our return to the United States, and she shared her overall impression of the trip as a success for Vice President Harris. "In every country, she was so intentional about what she wanted to accomplish, and I think she largely did that. Recognizing that she wasn't there to fix everything between the continent and the United States, but she was there as the highest profile member, so far, of the administration to say that they have an ongoing commitment to Africa. She was part diplomat, part stateswoman, and part saleswoman. We got to see all of that on display."[20] Haines said that she was also struck by the global reach of the vice president's message to seize the moment of possibility that exists for Africa beyond humanitarian efforts. "She shifted the tone and rhetoric in how world leaders talk about the continent. It felt very different."[21]

Haines also spoke to me about the perception of Vice President Harris as a global leader. "What we saw, starting with Ghana, was a huge example of her presence and her reception on the world stage," she said. "This trip felt momentous, an opportunity to really see her leading on the ground. How she was received and perceived and what she represents for people abroad and the people on the continent of Africa. In America, we don't tend to think of the vice president as someone who is particularly consequential, even though she is a historic figure. But abroad, she is a representative of the most powerful democracy in the world."[22] Haines said that, in talking to young girls on the continent about what the vice president's visit represented to them, they were most excited about the potential opportunities that she can bring to the continent and African countries, opportunities that could fundamentally change their lives.[23]

Voters in the US tend to qualify our leaders as having international credibility based on their travel and exposure abroad. Generally, abroad means any country other than your own, but in terms of American politics, travel to European countries typically carries more weight than exposure to areas of the world that have large populations of people of color. Under these standards, summers spent backpacking in Europe carry more credibility than studies on the continent of Africa. There is a pressure for international experiences to look one way, which tends to disqualify people of color. The makeup of the American diplomatic corps is, in part, an outgrowth of this paradigm. In one of her last acts as a member of the US House of Representatives, Los Angeles mayor Karen Bass co-sponsored a bill aimed at diversifying America's foreign services. The Diversity and Inclusion at the Department of State Act establishes the position of chief diversity officer within the office of the deputy secretary of state. It also requires that a substantial number of women and members of minority groups be appointed to the board of examiners and the foreign service selection boards, mandates diversity and inclusion training, adds diversity as a factor in promotions, and provides an annual senior executive candidate development program for the civil service.

"The State Department is America's face to the world and the workforce must represent the United States' commitment to diversity and inclusion in order to effectively advance American values on the world stage," said then congresswoman Bass when discussing the bill. "For years, the State Department has expressed a commitment to building a workforce that reflects the diverse composition of the United States. Since the State Department has been unable to act on workforce diversity, Congress intends to work with them to do so with this bill and others."[24]

In terms of background, credentials, and professional abilities, former president Trump and Vice President Harris could not be more different. You have a career prosecutor and sitting vice president who is embracing the African diaspora. A Black woman who is widening the lens, looking at the continent of Africa as more than public health and humanitarian opportunities. She is looking at opportunities to invest, to support entrepreneurship for folks that look like her—Black people, women, and people of color. On the other side, you have a former president who was ranked as the worst president in US history by a group of nonpartisan presidential historians. A man who referred to African countries as "shithole" countries. This is somebody who has caught several civil and criminal cases while out of office and even before getting in the office. Somebody who has had a series of entanglements with the justice system, and that's being polite about it. Yet, one of America's two major political parties deems him as an appropriate world leader while simultaneously characterizing Vice President Harris as incapable of representing America on the global stage.

The 2024 presidential election offers a choice between dueling worldviews, and the results will have a cascading effect across the continent of Africa and the African diaspora, which includes Black folks here in the United States. And the way that will look largely depends on which worldview wins in November 2024. When you have a former president whose pitch to Black folks consisted of "What do you have to lose," it falls on us to articulate what we have to lose across the diaspora. And I can't underscore those far-reaching consequences enough. It's not just about winning over Black folks in South Carolina; Black folks in Georgia; Black folks in Detroit, Philly, or Milwaukee. Yes, these are all very critical communities that went for the 2020 Biden-Harris ticket in battleground states, but it is even bigger than that. It's about leaning in and more clearly understanding the reach of our power. I don't know if Black folks are paying attention. It worries me that Black folks don't think about our agency and how we choose to assert it because I don't know if we even recognize that our agency means something to the lives of Black folks across the diaspora.

When the world saw the murder of George Floyd on video, that had a rippling effect. We saw folks across the diaspora, for example, protesting the murder of, the inhumanity, the indignity that George Floyd was subjected to. And if that experience could ripple across the African diaspora, imagine a more life-affirming, life-seeking, life-determining vision. Imagine how that might ripple across the continent. A lot of what Black folks in Ghana, Tanzania, and Zambia want is not all that different from what Black folks in Georgia, South Carolina, Michigan, and Pennsylvania want— human rights, access to capital, good paying jobs, and a family legacy to pass on to the next generation. We all want the ability to participate in a fair and just economy. Women don't want to be shut out of the opportunity to be a part of our economy in a real way. We all want to be safe and secure but not at the expense of our civil and human rights. Not at the expense of our civil liberties. When I heard the Zambian president respond to the question about Donald Trump's indictment by referring to the rule of law and its application across the board, without regard to whom the transgressor may be, it highlighted the similarities in what he wants for the people of his country and what we want as descendants of the diaspora living in America—equal justice under the law.

CHAPTER NINE

A SMALL FARM WITH A BIG MISSION

On April 1, 2023, we awoke early to visit a farm on the outskirts of Lusaka. I had no idea what kind of farm it would be because the only direction given to the press corps was to dress appropriately with long sleeves and pants and to put on our Deet. So, I followed directions and laced up my Adidas sneakers to go and visit a farm. Riding with the motorcade, I saw Zambian people standing along both sides of the street, cheering as the vice president passed by. I also noticed a number of billboards for Oriental Steel company. The Chinese writing on the advertisements stood out to me as an unexpected reminder of China's influence across the continent. As we pulled up to the farm, I looked around curiously, still with no idea what to expect. But it did not take long for Panuka Farm to make a real impression on me.

The vice president began her remarks by communicating her appreciation for the farm's name, which means "being clever." She asked, "… isn't that at the heart of what we want people to do? Which is to use our imagination, use our vision, and be encouraged to use it in a way that will inspire. And we'll do what we call 'innovate'—create new things, see what is possible, and then go and get it. And that's what the leaders here are doing."[1] She went on to speak about the importance of the work being done at the farm and its relevance to all nations of Africa, mentioning three countries and their troubling statistics in particular.

"In Somalia, which has a population—for the American journalists here—about the size of New York, 43,000 people died due to drought last year alone," she stated. "In Malawi, which is also about the size of New York in terms of the population, Tropical Cyclone Freddie caused over 500 deaths. In Nigeria, which as a country is about two-thirds of the population of the United States, more than 1.4 million people were displaced due to historic flooding. So, these are just some examples of the proportion of harm that is being experienced on this continent and as an example of what is happening around the world that must be addressed with creative solutions."[2]

She went on to discuss the importance of cultivating and growing public-private partnerships, combining the valuable resources needed to craft models of innovation. "This work, then, that we are doing with the private sector, as I announced yesterday, will—because of the work that I've done to help generate more than $7 billion in private sector commitments, will support climate resilience, adaptation, and mitigation. This includes commitments to support climate-smart agriculture; to increase access to financing and insurance, which is a very big deal to more, on this continent, than 116 million farmers, which is about half of the farmers on the continent."[3]

As the vice president ended her remarks and began fielding questions from members of the African press corps, I was surprised at the large number of questions that centered on climate change related concerns. Their inquiries confirmed that climate change isn't just some lefty, liberal issue. It is an issue affecting people around the world. What a powerful demonstration of climate resilience coming out of Zambia, of all places.

Climate Matters to Black People, Too

During the pandemic, we often heard the phrase, "When America catches a cold, Black people get pneumonia." As it relates to climate change, when the world catches a cold, Africa gets pneumonia. Despite being the least responsible continent for global warming, Africa is the most vulnerable to its adverse effects. The continent is warming at a rate faster than the global average. The relentless scorching of the land affects crops and livestock, furthering the issue of food security. Extreme heat waves have already become the norm, and heat-related illnesses are surging disproportionally through vulnerable populations. Africa's glaciers are on track to completely vanish by the 2040s. As a vital water supply, their disappearance threatens the availability of fresh water for millions of people, a problem that threatens stability as communities engage in conflict over scarce water supplies. When people cannot access food and water where they live, they start to migrate into other areas where necessities are available. On the continent, this may mean different tribes with different languages and customs, sharing a small space, creating a perfect scenario for conflict.

The health of people on the continent is also affected by the heat. Africa's recorded temperatures already approach the limits of survival and are projected to climb higher in the coming years. The elderly, people with preexisting conditions, and children bear the brunt of this dangerous reality. Each year between 2011 and 2020, an estimated 12,000 to 19,000 heat-related child deaths occurred in Africa.[4] Diseases like malaria and yellow fever are on the rise across a continent that bore 95 percent of global malaria deaths in 2022.[5]

Sadly, I recognize that some people, many people fail to recognize the urgency of climate change and its impact on the people of the continent. So, let's broaden the view to examine the ways that this pervasive problem will impact countries around the world.

The ecosystem is a delicate balance representing a complex network of nature's systems. The relentless heat of climate change is creating a desperate struggle for Africa's ecosystems, a risk that extends to countries around the world. The lush forests of the Congo suffer under stifling heat and drought, a problem that will be felt in the absence of wood; diamonds; gold; and coltan, which is a mineral used to make cell phones. The global demand for these resources consistently increases, but that demand will not be met as climate change continues to ravage Africa's valuable raw materials. The charred remnants of wildfires, fueled by dry conditions, provide a real time view of what's in store for rainforests of Africa as the effects of climate change worsen.

Rising seas encroach upon wetlands, swallowing whole them and the birds, amphibians, and aquatic plants they support. These natural wetlands serve as a type of flood control, and when they succumb to rising waters, they no longer serve as a buffer between cities and the seas. Migration patterns shift with animals moving to find higher grounds and cooler havens. Polar bears, with nowhere to go, die stranded on shrinking ice glaciers. Mass extinction looms for endangered species like rhinos, gorillas, and hosts of coral reefs and amphibians. Species like lions, elephants, and cheetahs have already lost vast amounts of their ranges due to climate change and habitat loss. If the world does not respond to climate change in a meaningful way, we risk losing species that call the Motherland home.

Doing the Work

Touring Panuka Farm was eye-opening for me. It was very neat and orderly, not at all like the picture I had in my head. Its crops include English cucumbers, sweet peppers, iceberg lettuce, sweet corn, broccoli, and cauliflower. It is run on 100 percent renewable energy and employs techniques like green housing, solar energy, and drip irrigation. While we were there, they were also in trials for migration to organic fertilizers and pesticides. For me, one of the most impressive parts of Panuka Farm's climate resilience work was their use of AI technology to create a stronger yield on their crops.

Bruno Mweemba, CEO of Panuka Farm, talked to us about their six-month graduate trainee program, a part of the company's corporate social responsibility model that trains fresh graduates from agricultural colleges and universities. The second cohort of trainees was there during our visit, learning among a workforce that is 95 percent composed of people from the surrounding villages. It is also made up of equal numbers of male and female employees. As we walked around and met some of the people doing this important work, I was struck by how many of them reminded me of my family on my father's side. Some of them looked like they could have been my aunties or my grandmother. To learn that these folks weren't just out there doing old school farming but utilizing technology in incredible ways, it just blew me away. I don't think any of us expected to see that level of advanced technology in that part of the world, and that is what I mean about reexamining our underlying assumptions about the continent of Africa. Panuka Farm perfectly underscores that point.

As described by Mweemba, the farm is a "'laboratory' to test and showcase the practical side of what green finance practitioners discuss in air-conditioned boardrooms." Mweemba has a Master of Philosophy in development finance from Nelson Mandela University in South Africa and an MBA in financial services from University of East London. He is also certified as an expert in climate renewable energy finance by Frankfurt School of Finance and Management in Germany and certified as an infrastructure project finance expert by Middlesex University London. This is somebody who got a lot of education outside of Zambia and made it his business to come back and build an innovative farm outside of Lusaka and put his skill and education to work for the people. I think that's incredible. It takes me back to the value of collective responsibility that I was raised with.

Whether you are near or far to the place you call home, there's still a responsibility that you have to improve the conditions and make it possible for other people to achieve their hopes and dreams and live out their God-given potential. Zambia is on a different part of the continent from my father's homeland of Ghana, but you still see that principle at work as a value that we, as Black people, are steeped in across the diaspora. It's at odds with rugged individualism and the concept of pulling yourself up by the bootstraps. This value is a value that may not do us any favors politically, but the value of collective responsibility may be just the thing that makes us that perpetual outsider.

Let me be clear. I am not a socialist. I don't think the vice president's a socialist. I don't think that Mweemba at Panuka Farm is a socialist. Unfortunately, there is something about invoking this idea of collective responsibility in a capitalist country and in capitalist systems around the world that immediately sounds like socialism. Perhaps social entrepreneurship is how we split the difference—how we use the principles of entrepreneurship to solve social problems. The field of entrepreneurship is broader than what people think because you could use entrepreneurship to just make a whole lot of money, or you can use entrepreneurship to make profit, improve the planet, and make a difference in the lives of everyday people. And so, when you find that Black folks and other folks of color often engage in entrepreneurial endeavors at higher rates, perhaps this is why.

Zambia is reported to be losing more than 700,000 acres of forests each year, and the leading driver is agriculture.[6] In the quest to increase yield, most farmers have resolved to land extensification by cutting more trees to create new fields. That unfortunately exacerbates deforestation. Penuka Farms has developed a way for emerging farmers to farm commercially in a small space without the need to cut more trees as a proxy to increase yields. Mweemba said that the vice president was particularly interested in the productivity of the farm's greenhouses. She also saw the efficiency of the farm's water use, which involves a combination of drip irrigation, the use of gravity, and an ongoing project towards rainwater harvesting from the roofs of greenhouse complexes. At Penuka, we got to see an emerging farming enterprise run completely off grid. Since 2017, the farm has been running on 100 percent solar power.

The vice president highlighted some of this important work in her remarks, stating "… a lot of what you're doing here is about high tech, using cellphone apps to track plant health, and using solar energy to power buildings and irrigation systems. Bruno showed me on his phone the app that he has been using over the last two years so that he can use the camera on his phone to take a picture of the leaf of a plant, and the app will then tell him, because of AI and what it has been programmed to do, 'Oh, there are certain kinds of infestation that are hurting that plant; that plant needs a certain kind of food to address whatever might be harming it; that plant needs less water, more water, less sun, less sun.'" She also talked about Penuka's reach beyond Zambia, particularly as it pertains to micro agriculture. "Here in Zambia, we know almost 80 percent of the farmers are women. And by providing microfinance—which is essentially access to capital—to help women start a farm, grow a farm, and increase not only the productivity in terms of the food production piece of it, but also increase the economic status of their families in their communities."[7]

Zambia is not alone in its environmental efforts. Many other African countries are also making concerted efforts to reverse the effects of climate change and transition towards low-carbon technologies. Morocco has built the world's largest concentrated solar facility to help achieve the country's goal of 52 percent renewable energy mix by 2030. The 6,000-acre solar complex serves as a clean energy source for around 2 million Moroccans as the country transitions away from the fossil fuel industry. In June 2019, South Africa's Carbon Tax Act came into effect with the goal of reducing the country's emissions by 33 percent relative to the baseline by 2035. South Africa's renewable energy auctions have resulted in solar and wind prices that are lower than those from new coal plants. Nigeria, a country that consistently struggles with the provision of electricity for a majority of its population, has set a renewable energy target of 30 percent by 2030, underscoring the potential for both grid-based and decentralized renewable energy investments to simultaneously deliver energy access and climate change benefits.

The African Development Bank is a finance institution that focuses on sustainable economic development and social progress of African countries. Its flagship climate initiatives support over 30 million farmers using data-driven services. They are also providing financial support for youth-led subject matter experts in climate resilience and identifying green investment markets to increase adaptation finance. Despite the portrayal of Africa as a continent in need of constant care and saving, its resilience shines through with the efforts being made across Africa to fight climate change and invest in renewable energy.

A Record to Stand On

The vice president could have chosen a public health or humanitarian oriented focus for this trip to Africa, just as so many world leaders before her have done. But instead, she emphasized global investment in the continent to include the innovative work being done to address climate change by African nations. A lot of people miss this nuance, but it is part of who the vice president has been as a champion for the environment. While serving as district attorney of San Francisco, she created an environmental justice unit to deal with environmental crimes. Speaking to the *San Francisco Chronicle* in 2005, she said "… crimes against the environment are crimes against communities, people who are often poor and disenfranchised."[8] As the junior senator from California, she championed the Water Justice Act, a bill aimed at addressing critical water-related issues across the nation to ensure that every American had access to safe, affordable, and sustainable water. She also co-sponsored multiple resolutions and bills focused on pollution reduction, wildlife conservation, and climate change mitigation. The League of Conservation Voters has given Vice President Harris a lifetime voting record of 90 percent pro-environmentalism, a score higher than President Biden who holds a lifetime score of 83 percent.[9]

Endless Potential

Africa is undeniably associated with rich cultural heritage and breathtaking landscapes, but its role in technological development has been greatly underreported. European nations have consistently upheld the myth that African nations are incapable of taking the lead in scientific innovation. This is another vestige of slavery and colonialism that elevates the contributions of European nations over those of African countries. The exploitation of the continent's natural resources left its nations with fragments of the wealth they should have amassed, which negatively impacted their ability to fund technological innovations. In addition, the arbitrary borders created by colonial rulers fueled ethnic tensions, driving wedges in spaces where cooperation and building could have occurred.

If responsibility for climate change determined which countries would do the heaviest lifting, then African countries absolutely would not carry that burden. But it must also be noted that the continent does bear some responsibility in the realm of governance. There is a history of African leaders allowing industries to come into their countries and do what they want free from regulation to the gain of individual African leaders in positions of power. And that certainly has not helped the situation that is currently unfolding. While I do not think this burden belongs solely on the shoulders of Africans, I also cannot deny the fact that some African leaders have been compromised by their narrow self-interest, an enrichment that has accelerated some of the negative effects of industry on the environment.

If fairness was the measure, countries like China, the US, India, and the EU would carry most of the burden as the world's largest contributors to climate change.[10] But we know that fairness rarely enters the conversation when European nations discuss the continent of Africa. So, despite the numerous factors standing in the way of progress, African countries continue to forge a way towards environmental responsibility.

There are many reasons why the continent has not taken its rightful spot as a leader in global technologies, but more conversation needs to occur around what the people of Africa are doing to drive environmental innovation. Yes, the continent's climate economy is headed in the right direction, but will Western nations support or frustrate these efforts? The potential is endless, and African nations are stepping up to the plate. Over 90 percent have ratified the Paris Agreement, and many countries have made commitments to transition to green energy. South Africa's Carbon Tax Act levies greenhouse gasses from fuel combustion and industrial emissions. And to paraphrase the vice president, a little farm in Zambia is creating new things, seeing what is possible, and going after it.

CHAPTER TEN

MISSED OPPORTUNITIES

Two Black female leaders standing together on a global stage. Thousands of young people packing into Black Star Square to hear an American leader speak. The vice president standing her ground and championing LGBTQ+ rights amid snickering and scorn. These are just a few of the important and newsworthy moments that were missed by the American press. Instead of covering the vice president's visit like the historic occasion that it was, the overwhelming majority of outlets gave it no more coverage than a brief restatement of the daily agenda.

While I might have expected that level of lackluster attention from mainstream media, I was highly disappointed by the absence of Black media outlets traveling with the press corps and frustrated with the lack of substantive coverage provided to Black folks back home. Even my own media home was unenthusiastic about recognizing the history-making significance of this momentous journey, and that speaks volumes about the current state of the American press and media landscape.

WHEN THE PRESS SPEAKS, DEMOCRACY LISTENS

Renowned abolitionist, writer, and orator Frederick Douglass once said, "Liberty is meaningless where the right to utter one's thoughts and opinions has ceased to exist. That, of all rights, is the dread of tyrants. It is the right which they first of all strike down. They know its power. Thrones, dominions, principalities, and powers, founded in injustice and wrong, are sure to tremble, if men are allowed to reason… Equally clear is the right to hear. To suppress free speech is a double wrong. It violates the rights of the hearer as well as those of the speaker." These words underscore the incredible power of the press to shape public opinion and advance the principles of democracy.

Journalism plays a fundamental role in safeguarding democratic principles by fostering an informed citizenry and holding a mirror of accountability up to political leaders. Any truly democratic society needs a free press to maintain the flow of accurate information that empowers citizens to actively participate in their own governance in an informed way. This is the profound responsibility and power that the press wields in shaping the fabric of America.

At any given time, democracy rests on the principles of transparency, accountability, and the free exchange of ideas. Without an independent press, these principles can quickly erode under the influence of political corruption. The "watchdog" powers of the press to scrutinize those in power and inform citizens about governmental wrongdoings get stripped away by force or coercion. The professional skills of investigative reporting and in-depth analysis of public affairs provide the public with something more valuable than a simple view of what's happening, but it also provides the complex nuances that far too many Americans miss in the current culture of social media "reporting." True journalists are the eyes and ears of the public, entrusted with the responsibility of challenging the powerful, amplifying marginalized voices, and advocating for everyday people. A robust and ethical press shines a critical light on government actions, policies, and decisions for the sole purpose of arming citizens with the straightforward information they need to be well-informed participants in the democratic system.

With the future of American democracy hinging on every presidential election cycle, I am also reminded of another important role that the press plays in maintaining democracy, which is the provision of an unbiased platform upon which diverse viewpoints and public debate can take place. The press is supposed to maintain an open forum for the exchange of ideas, viewpoints, and perspectives, which is essential to the fostering of civic engagement. Within a democracy, no single viewpoint should dominate the public discourse so that minority opinions can be earnestly considered. This is the only path to a society where all people feel heard.

Unfortunately, that path is being obstructed with the whirlwind of misinformation and disinformation that is currently occupying a dangerous amount of space within social media as well as the subset of news outlets that choose to value entertainment and dollars over truth. This pervasiveness of half-truths, alternative facts, and outright lies have the insidious ability to sow seeds of distrust and hatred among citizens, undermining people's faith in their democratic institutions and the credibility of even the legitimate press. The constant assault of conflicting narratives and falsehoods frustrate what little room they have in their busy lives for political analysis. As a result, they grow disillusioned with the governmental processes that affect them and their families on a daily basis. They either disengage from civic participation or fall prey to the manipulation of political actors seeking to exploit their lack of knowledge and vulnerabilities.

The lack of media literacy that we are witnessing in this country is extremely troublesome for me. What do I mean by that? I'm concerned that the skill set available in the public square, when it comes to quickly identifying misinformation and disinformation, is outdated. Our smartphones and devices have made us more interconnected, but they have also made it a lot easier for people to share information that may not be accurate. They can cherry pick an aspect of a story or an aspect of somebody's narrative to cast said individual as something that may fall short of who they really are, as something that they may not truly be.

On Martin Luther King Jr. Day 2024, almost a year after covering her in Africa, I covered the vice president for a campaign stop in South Carolina. We left the South Carolina

State House a little after one o'clock in the afternoon, and a half an hour later, we pulled up to Big T's Bar-B-Que where a few dozen supporters had gathered to greet the vice president, including Jaime Harrison, head of the Democratic National Committee, and a group of college students. Vice President Harris offered remarks about the vital role that South Carolina played in electing the 2020 Biden-Harris ticket, speaking extensively about issues facing families and communities in rural America. She also spoke about voting rights and reproductive rights, reinforcing her commitment to fight against attacks on "hard-won freedoms."

She closed her remarks with a focus on Generation Z, which prompted the group of young people to cheer and yell out "We love you, Kamala!" to which she responded with a big smile and joy in her voice, "I love Gen Z!" She then jokingly and humbly reminded the older folks in the audience that eighteen-year-olds were born in 2005. It was a lighthearted moment that showcased her personality and genuine connection with the younger generation. When the moment passed, the vice president returned to her remarks and talked earnestly about the weight of Gen Z's lived experiences as a younger generation having to navigate climate change, the George Floyd murder, active shooter drills, and the overturning of *Roe v. Wade*.

It was a routine campaign stop where she discussed substantive issues, yet two days later, while scrolling social media, a reel caught my eye. It was from the South Carolina stop, yet instead of highlighting what the event was or any of the discussed topics, the description read "Kamala can't stop laughing because she loves Gen Z." The clip showed only the part of her appearance where she was laughing and interacting with the young people in attendance. It also had this cartoon type of music in the background that seemed to insinuate that the vice president was either drunk or unintelligent. It was a very clear example of the power of misinformation and disinformation. The power of people to take a single moment of truth and use it to foment a suggestion that she is something that she is not.

As Black folks, it's nothing new to us because we see that game every day. How often have we seen Black men and women who are harmed at the hands of law enforcement, and when it goes to trial, they are essentially accused of doing it to themselves, bludgeoned by their own narratives in life and in death. So, if that can be true in the realm of criminal justice, imagine what's possible politically.

That's the importance of having media literacy. It provides a screen for us to absorb, digest, and critique news and information that may or may not benefit us as a people.

If a slim majority of us is fundamentally unskilled, inept, cavalier, and undiscerning in being media literate, then there's a residual effect in terms of how we view, support, and assess our leaders. And if that's off, then we can start to understand why folks across this country and Black folks across the diaspora might reach the conclusion that democracy may not be worth fighting for anymore. They may start to believe that dictators and authoritarian leaders may not be all that bad. We already know that the leadership of China has communicated to President Biden and others around the world that they're betting that authoritarian leadership is going to lead the century because of the quickness with which decisions are made with fewer people involved in the decision-making process. We also know that China has an increasing footprint across the continent of Africa and across the diaspora. But many of us fail to examine the vice president's trip to Africa in relation to these important aspects because we lack the media literacy to do so.

It is incumbent that more media outlets and professionals do more to promote media literacy because the purveyors of disinformation are using it to destroy the integrity of US elections by suppressing voter turnout and undermining the legitimacy of any election results that do not go in their favor. We have seen foreign adversaries take part in this madness by exploiting social media platforms to spread inaccurate information under false identities, to sow division, and influence the outcome of US elections as they have done to so many other fragile democracies around the world.

America is not separate and apart from the backsliding that we're seeing around the world when it comes to democracy. And one of the real questions that many people have right now is "What has democracy done for me lately?" If I'm sitting in Jackson, Mississippi or Flint, Michigan or any other part of the country where I feel forgotten and all I see on the news is talk about the economic growth and how well the economy is doing, I am probably wondering where this information is coming from because I am not feeling or seeing these economic gains. Democracy's inability to make a material difference in the lives of everyday people over time begins to undercut the very concept of democracy itself. The symbolism of showing up to rally folks around the idea of democracy and what it can be is important, but it's not enough. Just reporting that the vice president took an important trip to the continent is not enough. We need the media to ask the harder questions and make connections to what is important to Black folks across the diaspora. We, as citizens, need to ask those questions not just for the credibility of the vice president or the credibility of the Biden-Harris administration but for the credibility of democracy itself.

This current media landscape represents a red flashing light, not just in terms of who controls the House and the Senate and who occupies the White House, but it's a red flashing light for democracy itself. Any healthy democracy requires information that people can trust. We are living in an age with more broadcast, streaming, and digital channels than there have ever been in my lifetime. The competition for ratings and views has driven a willingness by the media to broadcast, share, and amplify content that inspires distrust of our institutions and one another. This flawed ethical decision-making framework, coupled with the ease of spreading misinformation and disinformation, has created a polluted media environment. This is about more than just conservative media versus liberal media. That is an over-simplification. The red flashing light for democracy is the possibility that in the near future, wherever people consume their news and information, they may be doing so in an era where they don't know who or what to trust. This is how the backsliding of democracy happens.

The addiction to confirmation bias and disdain for balanced discourse have led to a society where our divisions are exacerbated and made larger by the seemingly insurmountable polarization being fueled by toxic levels of partisan and sensationalized content. We are quickly descending into an echo chamber where any common ground escapes us and makes it impossible to reach any consensus on pressing societal issues. As a result, our democratic societies may become more susceptible to manipulation by extremist groups, demagogic leaders, and authoritarian regimes seeking to exploit social divisions for their own gain.

Our roles as journalistic watch dogs and the gatekeepers of democracy are constantly being undermined by the spread of disinformation. It is infuriating and heartbreaking for me to watch the basic journalistic standards of accuracy, fairness, and accountability get pushed aside in the race to capture the most clicks and generate the most advertising revenue. A symbiotic relationship exists between a healthy press and a healthy democracy. And as a professional journalist, I take my role as a guardian of public interest seriously, which is why I feel it is necessary to interrogate the role that the press chose to play in this extraordinary trip and how that coverage correlates to the state of the news media today.

I hope this book is a powerful demonstration of solutions journalism. As journalists, we talk a lot about what's wrong and what's not working. We don't talk enough about what's right, what is working, what's being tested. We don't kick the tires on things enough, at-large. We talk about challenges more than we talk about breakthroughs. And I hope that this book helps people to get beyond the challenges and gives them hope in real possibilities.

FIGHTING FOR A VOICE

The press is essential to any healthy democracy, and Black folks in the United States have not always been allowed the opportunity to fully participate in either. Like most of America's historic institutions, the mainstream media has deeply rooted systems of bias and discrimination that have persisted for centuries, resulting in the exclusion of Black voices, diverse perspectives, and culturally relevant stories from their coverage. Though great strides have been made, the roots of exclusion hold strong, resulting in limited employment opportunities for Black journalists, biased reporting that prefers the "entertainment value" of perpetuating negative stereotypes, and a lack of comprehensive coverage of issues relevant to Black communities.

Founded in early nineteenth century New York City, *Freedom's Journal* pioneered the voice of Black journalism. The weekly newspaper was founded by John Russwurm and Samuel Cornish, two prominent Black activists. The articles, editorials, poems, and narratives published by *Freedom's Journal* challenged the prevailing narratives that loudly dominated the conversations around race and slavery at the time. The paper gave Black folks a platform to tell their own stories. Russwurm and Cornish understood the important role of the press in educating Black people about the country in which they lived. *Freedom's Journal* and the Black press that followed have consistently had to punch above their weight class to just exist.

In the 1890s, through her powerful writing, Ida B. Wells used the power of the press to launch an anti-lynching campaign. A formerly enslaved woman who stood less than five feet tall, Wells pioneered reporting techniques that remain central tenets of journalism today. She put her investigative journalism skills to work, boldly challenging the mainstream narratives that portrayed lynching victims as criminals deserving of punishment.

The images of Gordon Parks put faces to the stories of racial discrimination and the fight for civil rights. The first Black man to work at *Life* magazine, Parks spent two decades covering subjects ranging from racism and poverty to fashion and entertainment. He took some of our most cherished photographs of Black icons like Muhammad Ali, Malcolm X, and Stokely Carmichael.

On New Year's Day 2006, trans activist and journalist Monica Roberts introduced TransGriot to the world, a blog dedicated to chronicling the stories of Black trans people. Roberts filled a void in the journalism space around issues that mattered to Black trans people and other trans people of color. She fought unapologetically against misgendering in the media and never backed away from her mission, even if it meant challenging the discomforts of others.

These media pioneers boldly stepped forward to give a voice to the Black community, and that same sense of urgency remains for the investment in more Black press. There's a lot of support for influencers, and it's great that they have a space in the ecosystem. But in this age of misinformation and disinformation, it is vitally important to have Black members of the press who can discern and sort through what's fact and what's fiction. We need journalists who not only recognize the nuance that exists in issues that impact our community but who also have the ability to do the code switching that is necessary to gather accurate information and bring it to the Black community in a way that gets attention.

Think back to the darkest days of COVID-19. One of the things that we quickly found out is that Black folks weren't trusting the information they were getting. They didn't know if they could believe the white elected officials and doctors who appeared on their televisions each day with COVID-19 updates. The most trusted professionals became Black doctors, nurses, and medical professionals who were in high demand. This is why the Black press is essential to an informed Black electorate. And in the seminal moment of the first Black vice president of the United States visiting the continent of Africa, there was not nearly enough Black press at the table. This trip offered an extremely rare opportunity to interrogate those big questions that prompt meaningful discussions about the woman behind the title of vice president. Her decision to go on this trip and her showing up on the continent in the way that she did opened the door for a series of conversations around those things that connect us to her, the people of Africa, and the people of the African diaspora. But these conversations do not happen unless organizations that exist to support Black journalists, like the National Association of Black Journalists (NABJ), are a part of the discussion. Maybe one Black news outlet did not have the financial ability to send a journalist on a major trip like this, but if more Black-led and Black-serving outlets pooled their collective resources, perhaps they could have sent one more person to report for more outlets. Organizations like the NABJ have tirelessly advocated for diversity and equity in newsrooms, while the very few independent Black-owned media outlets that we have continue working to amplify Black voices and stories.

With all that I went through to be a part of this journey, I should not have had to make a case for covering this historic trip. Black journalists, in general, should not have had to make a case for covering this historic trip. We've got to ask ourselves why Black journalists are interrogated about the value of covering Vice President Harris on a historical trip to Africa with questions like "Are we getting an exclusive? Is she going to do this? Is she going to do that?"

Why wasn't there sufficient interest in covering this on its face? Was it because Vice President Harris was the focus? Was it because of the locations? Was it because of the cost? Was it because you believe that your viewers, listeners, readers, and consumers don't care? Is it because the editorial class has already decided what the dominant narratives will be about the sitting vice president, and a trip like this is at odds with the narratives that they've already deemed acceptable? Let's take it even further. Is the press even equipped to cover a principle that is not just Black but a Black mixed-race woman? Is the press even equipped to cover a US vice president who looks vastly different from any vice president who came before her? A lot of people think that the demographics of America are shifting, and the future of this country looks a lot like Kamala. But at what point will the future of the press match that shift? And what are the consequences if it doesn't in terms of providing folks with the historical context and the connection to community?

Don't tell me that viewers don't care and then walk away as if powerless because media outlets actually possess a great deal of power over what consumers choose to care about. Let's explore two schools of thought on this. There are some who say that the press has the power to not just say that Black lives matter but to make Black lives matter through human interest. To make Black lives matter by helping folks to understand the direct line between the past, the present, and the future. Then, there are other people who say "Well, that's editorializing. That's opinion journalism."

Being a Black gay man with academic credentials and experience on the other side of the table as an advocate, I have characteristics that make me a better journalist. And I am professional enough and mature enough to recognize when those credentials and that expertise are pulling focus from my subject and from my objectivity. I think there are some who believe that, quite frankly, if you're from a traditionally marginalized group or a number of groups or if you have had an unconventional path to this work, that, somehow, you're not able to do the job as well as people who had a more conventional path, folks who have less of a connection or a relationship in the orbit of what or who they're covering.

This is the importance of having not just more Black folks in front of the camera, not just more Black media platforms, but having more Black professionals in positions of leadership and in positions of editorial power.

I recall one FOX SOUL team member giving feedback to me and my co-anchor during a team meeting. As co-anchors, we got a lot of feedback about what we were wearing, our makeup, how we were connecting or not connecting, our chemistry, and all sorts of things. They said to my co-anchor, "You come off as sort of hip hop and fried chicken, and Nii-Quartelai comes off as jazz and sushi." I was speechless, and I don't even think they were aware of how that came off, how limiting and offensive it was to share that kind of feedback at all, let alone on a team call. But it's an experience I never forgot because it was another reminder of the limitations that our people can put on ourselves in terms of what Blackness is, what it means to be rooted in your Blackness, what it means to be rooted in our culture.

It's not lost on me that the experience that I had is likely not all that different from some experiences that Kamala may have had throughout her career and certainly during her vice presidency. It's so important that we challenge ourselves and challenge one another to widen the lens in terms of what experiences we are willing to validate and what experiences we prefer to invalidate.

The experience I had as a co-anchor was jarring because it was like, "Wait a minute. I'm co-anchor on a daily news show called *Black Report*. Isn't the whole idea to take our viewers on a journey across what's happening in Black America every day?" So, if we are being true to that, we do that through a wide lens and not a narrow lens. We had many conversations about including stories on the show that were very heavy on what I used to call murder, murder, kill, kill, stab, stab. And before you deliver the news, you experience the news. You feel the news. At least that was what I experienced. And when you read enough murder, murder, kill, kill, stab, stab stories, you might find yourself getting a little weepy with a sense of despair. As journalists, I believe we have a responsibility to counteract these stories by providing viewers with a wider lens.

So, as exciting as it is to see more Black media platforms and more Black people in media as journalists, contributors, and subject matter experts, we can't take our foot off the gas in terms of pushing for more Black folks and people from other traditionally marginalized backgrounds in leadership roles. Audiences fail to recognize that just because you are an anchor, it doesn't mean that you have the final word in terms of what goes to air. Part of the brilliance and legacy of trusted and respected journalists like Gwen Ifill, Dan Rather, Tavis Smiley, Peter Jennings, and Diane Sawyer is the fact that they weren't just anchors or reporters; they were also managing editors, which means that they had a heavy hand in terms of how those programs and the news was shaped.

Now, for the naysayers in the back, let me be clear that I'm not suggesting that only Black journalists should be covering Black elected officials or Black subjects. What I am suggesting is that when you are of the community and have a level of immersion in the community, there is a language that you understand, a kinship, a relationship, an orbit that you are a part of, which is fundamentally valuable when it comes to sorting out fact from the fiction, processing out the misinformation and disinformation, and getting to the heart of any story. That should be valued much more than it currently is, and when we have to put up a losing fight to cover stories like the vice president's trip, the narratives that emerge seem to be very narrow. When none of the people covering our communities have the lived experience of being the perpetual outsider, as so many Black folks, women folk, queer folk, and folks from traditionally marginalized communities have, we cheat our audiences, and we cheat our communities from the opportunity to know better and do better.

MUCH REQUIRED

At this very minute, I can almost guarantee you that my mom's television is toggling between MSNBC and CNN. She may accidentally land on FOX News and realize her mistake. But that TV is eventually going back to MSNBC.

So, when you examine what assumptions the media have instilled in you about Vice President Harris, start by looking at your media diet. There is nothing wrong with fast food, but if you eat it every day out of the week, it is probably not going to be good for your health. You are not maximizing the nutritional value that your body needs. Similarly, if you are not thoughtful about your media consumption and critical about the sources of that media, you may end up consuming a lot of things that are not fundamentally good for you. You may be consuming media that make you anxious or that cause you to feel anger. It may cause you to feel depressed or isolated from your community. You may become more cynical in terms of your politics that, ultimately, becomes unhealthy for not just you but unhealthy for our democracy.

From my perspective, as a member of the media, I was raised to believe that to whom much is given, much is required, and these microphones have power. When you are given the opportunity to speak truth to power and communicate to the masses, you should do so with care and subscribe to the Hippocratic oath of doing no harm. That means exercising restraint and doing your due diligence, double- and triple-checking your work to ensure that the information you provide to people will allow them to make the best decisions for themselves. There should be a code of ethics for anyone who has the privilege of being able to communicate to the masses. But until that is a mandate, we all have to operate with the honor system. I want to do my part to make sure that I am doing the honorable thing when it comes to sharing information, and I think that is the best thing we can all do. Be a consistent, positive, and thoughtful demonstration of handling information with care. But people also have to put their money where their mouth is by investing in media platforms that are doing that. As long as folks invest in platforms that peddle in the most salacious and diminishing content about our communities, there is no incentive for them to do it differently.

So, I challenge you to become more aware of what media you are consuming and exercise your agency in terms of what sources you subscribe to, what individuals you follow. Read the entire article before you retweet or repost. Look at the date, and consider the source. Just those little steps can go a long way in strengthening your media literacy.

Erykah Badu imparted a wisdom on us that her granny imparted on her. She said, "Pick your friends like you pick your fruit." Well, pick your media like you pick your fruit.

CHAPTER ELEVEN

NO ESCAPE HATCH

A s I complete this book, America is preparing for what is probably the most consequential election of my lifetime. Much is at stake, and as I look forward to what the morning after the November 5, 2024 US national election may look like, I am more than a bit concerned for myself and my family. My communities. My birth country and my ancestral country. The weight of this election is part of what compelled me to share this incredible adventure, and I want folks to really interrogate their ideas about who people think Vice President Harris is versus the vice president I observed on this trip. The rigor that I'm bringing to telling this story is not disconnected from the rigor that people need to have as we come up on an election that raises serious questions about all our futures.

We each go to the ballot box with our own interests and concerns, including the pain points that drive our political decisions. For me, safety is a concern, and sadly, at home and abroad, I'm not alone. I don't mean to seem panicked or paranoid, but I think about safety and longevity knowing one cannot enjoy the benefits of longevity without enjoying some level of physical and psychological safety. On the last day of Black History Month 2024, I learned that after months of debate, Ghana's parliament approved the highly controversial anti-LGBTQ bill that was referenced during that joint press conference with Vice President Harris and Ghanaian president Nana Akufo-Addo. According to CBS News, "The Human Sexual Rights and Family Values bill is now one of the toughest pieces of anti-LGBTQ legislation in Africa.… Under the new law, [the] maximum sentence will increase [from three] to five years [in prison]."[1] Identifying as LGBTQ and funding LGBTQ work could also land you in prison if convicted. "It would bring in a custodial sentence for people convicted of advocating for LGBTQ rights and make distribution of material deemed supportive of LGBTQ rights illegal."[2] This extremist legislation fundamentally undermines the human rights of LGBTQ Ghanaians and allies. Its legislative intent is at odds with the beacon of hope Ghanaian democracy has been across the Black diaspora.

Meanwhile, at home in the United States, NBC recently reported that, according to FBI data, the number of reported hate crime offenses across all categories increased from almost 8,500 in 2018 to over 13,000 in 2022 with the most common location being residential settings followed by those occurring on highways, roads, and alleys.[3] Schools, colleges, and universities represent the third most common locations. As a public figure who travels pretty frequently coast to coast, as somebody who has a home in a residential setting, as somebody who is Black and openly gay, as somebody who is not just a journalist but a professor, I can't help but feel highly vulnerable to these dangers. I think about that a lot and not just my safety but the safety of my husband who also frequently travels as a reality television producer and may be a little less passing than myself. If you see me in an airport, you may not right away clock all my identities, but there are folks out there, like my husband, where you might quickly clock them. I'd like to think I have a healthy fear, that I'm not overtaken by but depending on what's trending in the news, and I do sometimes worry about receiving a phone call that someone I care about has been the subject of a hate crime. Whoever occupies the White House at the end of this election cycle, whatever movement prevails, will either add oxygen to this fear or quell it a bit.

This election is more than a contest around which policies will deliver more for everyday people. Of course, making material differences in the lives of people is extremely important, but this election is also about standards. It's also about what's socially acceptable and socially unacceptable. What's culturally acceptable and what's culturally unacceptable. As I read reports about the motivations behind these crimes, I don't have to wonder who these folks are. It's me and people like me. It's folks that I'm in community with and their family members.

Are we going to be a nation, though imperfect, that continues to make equal justice under the law, our North Star, or not? Are we going to be a nation that looks at the Civil

Rights Act and the Voting Rights Act and the Fair Housing Act as landmark pieces of legislation that should be celebrated and upheld in our highest court of the land? Or are we going to be a nation that sees those landmark pieces of legislation as the subject of our discontent and will, thus, do everything we can to dismantle them? Are we going to be a nation that finally delivers meaningful police reform? Or are we going to be a nation that turns a blind eye to the indifference of some law enforcement officials across the country when it comes to Black lives? This is not an academic exercise. These are issues that hit very close to home, and unlike some Black folks, I don't necessarily know where the escape hatch lies.

I have friends and colleagues who readily talk about moving to the continent of Africa depending on the results of this election. I hear that, and I think, "Okay. That is clearly their escape hatch, and it could possibly be mine, too; but that would likely require my being a muted version of myself in most places across the continent and the Black diaspora for that matter. If I were closeted and if I didn't attempt to write bestselling books and if I didn't provide analysis and commentary in very public forums that are rooted in the truth of who I am...then maybe that could be my escape hatch, too, but that is highly unlikely."

Still, the questions remain, "Where do I go? Where do we go?" We don't. We stay and fight for the country that my ancestors built. I think that's where I've landed. I am the son of a very proud African man who was born into colonialism, whose people fought for their independence and who enjoyed that independence. I am the son of one of the daughters of the civil rights movement whose early years dovetailed with the implementation of *Brown v. Board of Education*. Parents who were born an ocean apart and fell in love at an HBCU in Texas. Parents who, like so many other Black families, moved to California as part of the big western migration for job opportunities and safety. They settled in the Bay Area where I was born many years later. My story is the fabric of America, and so I very much feel like this land is my land. This land is my portion, and this fight is my fight. Even if I had an escape hatch, given the history that I carry, I am likely not the type to reach for that hatch without putting up a fight.

My parents taught me courage just by being themselves, and I love them for that. I come from a long line, on both sides, of people summoning the courage to wade through the moment to do their part in engineering a breakthrough. And I feel an incredible sense of responsibility to that history. And I know that I'm not alone. I think there are so many folks who are going to read this book who feel that same tension between that responsibility that we carry and what I hope is a healthy fear of the darkness.

Black people have a long history of erring on the side of their pragmatism, even in the face of bewilderment. And I think this time is no different. The fog from the pandemic has not completely lifted. We are working differently. We move through the world differently, and we never really grieved the one million deaths of our fellow Americans. And we know that Black folks, Black communities were some of the hardest hit during the darkest days of the pandemic. But there is also the grief of seeing our Black boys and men killed or harmed at the hands of law enforcement. How many more stories do we have to read about the disparity in consequences for Black people facing the same allegations that we see of white people? Think about what that means in terms of not just our economic security but our mental health and wellness.

Now, add the fact that any Diversity, Equity, and Inclusion gains we made in 2020 are being rolled back in every single possible way. Conservative political leaders are waging a war against diversity and equity by bullying leaders in the private sector to fall back and bullying leaders of academic institutions to fall back or to be taken out. Edward Blum, the same man whose lawsuit resulted in the US Supreme Court striking down the use of racial preferences in college admissions, turned his vitriol on the Fearless Fund, a venture capital fund that invests in businesses led by women of color, claiming that their program engages in "explicit racial exclusion."[4] We've seen a federal civil rights complaint filed against a George Floyd Memorial Scholarship, alleging that it violates Title VI of the Civil Rights Act by exclusively awarding funds to Black students.[5] After the tragic collapse of Baltimore's Francis Scott Key Bridge, we saw racist social media attacks referring to the city's duly elected Black mayor as a "DEI mayor."

If this war on diversity can keep public scholars like Nikole Hannah-Jones from tenure at places like The University of North Carolina at Chapel Hill and relentless work to unfairly remove Dr. Claudine Gay from her position as president of Harvard University—if all of that is possible, then do we really think that folks are fairly assessing the performance of our vice president?

These people earned extraordinary credentials, and I very intentionally use the word "earned" because nobody was gifted them at all. If we understand that our credentials won't save us, our Black excellence alone will not save us. If that's the experience of Black people each and every day, then our understanding around critiques of our vice president cannot be divorced from the unfairness that we see in terms of how we are all assessed because we are Kamala and Kamala is us. That is not to say that we all score a perfect one hundred on every single assessment. This is not a critique against critique. I believe critique is healthy. But there is a difference between fair critique and critique motivated by bias, critique motivated by bigotry, critique motivated by narrow political interests or self-interest. I'm advocating for fair and honest critique for Black leaders, for Black people in positions of power, influence, and authority, particularly in roles and in spaces that have historically excluded our people.

Again, it comes back to one of the many gems that the incomparable Toni Morrison left us with, the omnipresence of the white gaze. I suspect that we have a number of leaders, people in positions of power, influence, and authority inside and outside of government who are sometimes overwhelmed by that white gaze, and they sometimes succumb to the pressure of that gaze. They may buckle in the face of the white gaze or be seduced into seeking the approval of those with the white gaze. I think any Black person or person from a traditionally marginalized group has had to contend with that at some time or another as a legacy of the white supremacy ideology. If we all have to guard against that, then we have to ask ourselves how we are supporting our leaders in guarding against that as well? Our analysis is fundamentally incomplete if we're not interrogating our relationship, our proximity to the weight that we give to the white gaze, and that is inclusive of, but not limited to Vice President Kamala Harris.

One of the things that many of us may have in common with the vice president is the opportunity to be a bridge, figuratively, over troubled water. This is a time for bridge building, and the vice president's trip was a powerful demonstration of what that can look like. It takes time and effort, though. And building a bridge in the face of economic headwinds, social anxiety, racism, sexism, ageism, homophobia, and all forms of bigotry...it is not for the faint of heart. Bridge builders are change makers, and I don't think they get nearly enough credit. We live in a time where provocateurs get the attention, and because of that, our instincts sometimes tell us to throw it all away. If the bridge is incomplete, let's just blow it up and throw it all away.

Having grown up in the Bay Area, I remember a time before the new Bay Bridge was created. Long before earthquake standards were enacted, there was an old Bay Bridge that worked okay until 1989 when a section of the upper deck tragically collapsed. They needed to upgrade and build a stronger bridge that was earthquake proof, but they did not throw away the entire bridge. Instead, they recycled pieces of the old Bay Bridge into the new Bay Bridge. We live in a time where folks want to throw away the whole bridge, but we need to fight that urge.

THE VICE PRESIDENT VS. THE VICE PRESIDENCY

Though the Democratic Party has done a less than stellar job of pairing the accomplishments of the Biden-Harris administration with real stories of impact in the community, there have been and continue to be significant gains being made, and a lot of that legislative agenda would not have happened without Kamala casting the deciding vote. She has cast more tie-breaking votes than any other vice president in the history of the United States, and without that, Democrats across the country would not have nearly as much on which to campaign. This is not trivial and surely should not be taken for granted.

I think that there may be folks in the White House with a very old school approach to what it means to be a governing partner. Some might think that if the vice president shines too brightly, then her light may dim the halo around the president. It goes back to her being the perpetual outsider serving with a president who is firmly an insider, which means that a lot of the people who have worked with him over the years are also insiders. Whether we're talking about the White House or Washington, DC or any center of power, I don't know many insiders who willingly seed ground to people they perceive as outsiders. So, when I say we are Kamala and Kamala is us, this is one of the dynamics that we have to consider with grace.

During our interview, Dr. Frederick of Howard University spoke about the fallacy of underestimation around Vice President Harris. "It is interesting that the first Black woman vice president has such a level of expectation. It does not make sense to me. We have never had another vice president in this country that we have pushed so many expectations upon. That keeps being part of the discussion, and it should not be. That role is limited in some ways, and it requires some discipline. I think she has done exactly that and done what she was asked to do. This trip was another example of her executing an assignment to make it clear to Africa that America was there as an ally and substantively what America was prepared to do as an ally. She delivered on that."[6]

I strongly believe that folks conflate the vice president with the vice presidency. When then presidential candidate Joe Biden and vice presidential candidate Kamala Harris were running for the White House, some people supported that ticket expecting that she would be a full-throated public voice for Black folks and women. Once they got elected and started governing, reality set in, and some people were disappointed to see the vice president exhibit loyalty to President Biden. But here is the problem with that. Many people don't understand what the office of the vice president is. It's a unique office with an ambiguous type of role, which makes it subject to the whims of the president. That has been the case from the very first US vice president. But now that role is filled by a woman for the first time, a Black woman for the first time, and the expectations of the office are suddenly higher than ever before. The office of the vice presidency is not the office of the co-presidency. And I think there are folks who explicitly and implicitly carry the expectation that this president and vice president govern as co-presidents. That's not the deal. Nor has it ever been the deal, to my knowledge, when it comes to the offices of the president and the vice president. Regardless of how many glass ceilings she shattered and how great of a leader she is, she is still vice president. She is number two to the president, and her job is to support Biden. Folks have to be more realistic about what the office entails. Yes, she can get a lot done and move the ball forward on some issues, but she is still number two.

Now, this is not to say that the vice president, like other vice presidents, doesn't have areas of expertise that are helpful to advancing the president's agenda. For example, according to the Associated Press, "the longstanding concerns about President Joe Biden's age and memory intensified...after the release of a special counsel's report investigating his possession of classified documents. The report described the 81-year-old [president's] memory as 'hazy,' 'fuzzy,' 'faulty,' 'poor' and having 'significant limitations.' It noted that Biden could not recall defining milestones in his own life, such as when his son Beau died or when he served as vice president."[7] Biden responded to the report during a late-night press conference at the White House where he asserted that his memory was fine and was visibly angry as he denied forgetting when his son died.

The next day, Vice President Harris defended President Biden, calling the report "gratuitous, inaccurate, and inappropriate."[8] She went on to criticize the integrity exemplified by the special counsel. "The way the president's demeanor in that report was characterized could not be more wrong on the facts and clearly politically motivated. ... And so, I will say that when it comes to the role and responsibility of a prosecutor in a situation like that, we should expect that there would be a higher level of integrity than what we saw."[9]

That statement would not have hit the same if not for the vice president's experience as a prosecutor, if not for her relationship with the president. All vice presidents defend their presidents, but that response was a function of her expertise and her experience, not a function of the office. When I make the distinction between the vice president and vice presidency, that is what I mean.

Narrative change, culture change, and political change are woven together like the three parts of a French braid. Fairly or unfairly, the demands of the modern vice presidency coupled with expectations from voters who entrusted her to be a trusted voice expect that she weave these elements of social change like no other woman in the history of our country. Simply put, to whom much is given, much is expected, especially when you are a historic first. From the beginning of the transatlantic slave trade, Black people have been at the forefront of narrative change, culture change, and political change in this country. This moment is no different. We have to be conscious of the narratives and the cultural bear traps that are being laid before us. We must be conscious of our collective political power and the efforts being made to dilute that power, which includes discrediting the leaders whom we support.

In Her Words

This final section is an interview that I conducted with Madame Vice President at the conclusion of writing this book. I thought it was important to give her the final word so that you, the reader, can experience her humanity, personality, and tenacity for yourself. In this age of misinformation, disinformation, and distortion, whenever we give people an opportunity to show up authentically, we all stand to benefit.

NQQ: All right, Madam Vice President. It is good to see you. Thank you so much for this interview. For Americans that don't follow international affairs closely at a very high level, can you tell us how you would define US-Africa interest and why should Americans care about what's happening in Africa?

KH: Well, let's start with this. The median age on the continent of Africa is nineteen. By the year 2050, it is estimated that one in four people occupying space on Mother Earth will be on the continent of Africa. So, understand, then, that as much as anything, I believe the future of the world will be determined or largely influenced by what happens on the continent of Africa.

Number two, as vice president, I feel very strongly that we have to update, if not change, the narrative around how we think about the continent in that yes, there is good work that has happened to address global public health issues, what needs to be done in terms of dealing with child poverty and a number of those things. But also let us understand the extraordinary innovation and the dynamic nature of what is happening on the continent. And understand that we should think of our relationship with the continent and with the countries on the continent not as our benevolence in terms of aid but how we can partner, not what we're doing for the continent but what we're doing with the continent. So, I purposely curated my trip to the continent in a way that was very intentional about highlighting the incredible innovation and work that is happening there—in particular, among young entrepreneurs—to highlight this very point, and I purposely then curated the trip such that I would bring members of the diaspora along to emphasize the intertwined history between the United States and the continent and doing that with a vision toward also what will be an intertwined relationship for the future.

NQQ: Speaking about the intertwined relationship, Madam Vice President, to be a bit more pointed, what's at stake for Black Americans and people of African descent around the world if we ignore Africa?

KH: Well, first of all, we ignore Africa at our own peril for a number of reasons. I would say that, regardless of someone's race or where they live, if you have any interest as a leader, in the next twenty, fifty years out, you ignore Africa at your peril. And this is a fact. There's a lot of how I think about public policy—be it domestic or global—that is in the context of thinking about the future. Let us not just be burdened by tradition or by the crisis of the moment. Let us also think about what we are doing to pave a path toward a future that enhances security and prosperity for all. Because, by the way, there is also a national security reason to be invested in the prosperity of the continent. There is a reason to understand that the climate crisis is a crisis that has hit all of us but not so equally in terms of the impacts. But, where those impacts are not being addressed, you're going to see massive migration around the globe and potentially an uptick in conflict as a result of the fact that people move from the place where they speak the language and go to a place that speaks a different language and may pray to a different god.

But on the piece about people of African descent around the world—be it in the Americas, the Caribbean—what we know is that there is a shared history and, frankly, an emotional connection that we all have to the continent, and depending on who we are, that connection is very strong, especially when we are aware of our history and, therefore, also understand those who are trying to cover up or ignore or overlook.

NQQ: What should voters who care about Africa expect if former president Trump returns to the Oval Office?

KH: I just think of that beautiful thing that Maya Angelou gave us years ago. When people tell you who they are, listen to them the first time. He is the one who talked about s-hole countries. He has so clearly expressed an intent toward not supporting international rules and norms. He has a perspective that is that of an isolationist. And all Americans should be concerned about that because do understand—isolation does not equal insulation. The 1930s taught us quite well—when America withdraws from its alliances and partnerships, the threat will visit itself upon us. We are stronger when we are a leader in building and fortifying alliances and partnerships. I think about the partnerships that I've been working on on the continent—and you witnessed three of them—and what that does to further American interests, including economic interests, including our interest in partnering around innovation and technology in building clean energy economies, around how that will then allow us to mitigate against the harms of the climate crisis. I think about the continent of Africa in the context of meetings I have with American CEOs, letting them know that I am expecting that they will fortify public private partnerships that I'm creating with an understanding that as vice president, I will also sit down with these world leaders and talk about the importance of fighting against corruption, the importance of upholding rule of law, the importance of dealing with humanitarian issues, such as, for example laws against LGBTQ people and why that is going to be important for American business interests because, if nothing else, their employees and shareholders want to know that they're doing business with a country that upholds certain standards.

NQQ: Speaking of world leadership, I want to transition to some of our global alliances. The world is a complicated place, and international challenges abound. What can you tell me about your approach to world leadership and world affairs in spite of growing threats related to democracy, misinformation, and disinformation?

KH: I believe that America must always value and work to strengthen our alliances and partnerships. Again, I will say isolation does not equal insulation, and one of the first priorities that I have as vice president of the United States is America's security. To isolate ourselves from those relationships is to threaten our international security. My perspective is that we must be a defender and a coalition builder around international rules and norms, such as sovereignty, territorial integrity. My perspective is that we must be future forward thinking and figure out how we can see the capacity of these various nations and do our part to help invest in a way that strengthens democracies. It is a reality that when I look at, for example, the work I've done around the northern part of Central America, the irregular migration that we saw coming from that area, we've seen diminish, and there is a correlation between that and the billions of dollars that, through public private partnerships, I've been able to get to go into things like digital inclusion, supporting farmers, and getting people into online banking. It actually was very much a model for my approach to what we're doing on the continent of Africa. There is not a business anywhere in the world at this point, for the most part, that if it has a future, it's not a technology business. So, people need to be online. Digital inclusion should be one of our highest priorities. Undergirding almost every initiative that I have begun has been the digital inclusion piece.

NQQ: In a previous interview I did for this book, I spoke with former Howard University president Dr. Frederick. He said, quote, "It's interesting that the first Black woman vice president has such a level of expectation. It does not make sense to me. We have never had another vice president in this country that we've pushed so many expectations upon, that keeps being a part of the discussion, and it should not be." Madam Vice President, how do you manage the onslaught of expectations projected upon you at home and abroad?

KH: I feel a profound sense of duty, being the first, to ensure I won't be the last, and I am very acutely aware that my presence and the work that I'm able to do will impact people I'll never meet around the world. Doing the work on the continent, for example, focusing on issues like women's economic empowerment, focusing on young technologists, focusing on farmers who are engaged in smart farming techniques—that's going to have generational impact. And when I think of myself as a history maker, it is not only because of my race and my gender but because I have always believed in challenging the status quo and not being burdened by tradition if there's a better way of doing things.

NQQ: Starting with the 8,000 mostly young people that came out to hear you speak at Black Star Square in Ghana, it's clear there's a lot of young people that see you as a possibility model. What advice would you offer to existing and emerging leaders to meet the moment without sacrificing their mental health? It's a very polite way of saying how do you remain wrapped in your right mind?

KH: That's fair. So, the first thing that I'm going to say may be contrary to the point, but I'm gonna make it anyway because it's a fact. Breaking barriers. Breaking barriers is not starting on one side of the barrier, and you just end up on the other side. Breaking is involved, and when you break things, you get cut and you bleed. It is worth it every time, but it is not without pain. That is just the nature of it.

The second point is to not lose your mind ... and I wish I could talk to all our young people in more direct ways and more frequently than I'm able .... It is very important to make choices and be intentional about who you surround yourself with. Know that you have choices about who your friends are and who you choose to spend time with. Choose to spend your time and develop your relationships with people who encourage you, who applaud your ambition, who will be honest with you. People who, when you fall down, will laugh with you and then they will pick you up and push you back out. Because none of us, and I speak for myself, has achieved any level of success without those people in our lives. You can't do this kind of thing alone. It's almost impossible. So, a very important piece of advice that I offer is to choose to surround yourself with those people, and it's your power—you have the right. But, know that it's always gonna be worth it, but it's not gonna be easy; and then, just leave the door open.

NQQ: Last year, while on the ground in Africa, you committed the US to about $8 billion in public private partnerships. You and your team haven't stopped building upon these commitments ahead of the Kenya state visit. Can you share the theory of the case and preview what the administration is planning to deepen these Africa-wide commitments?

KH: The theory of the case is that, through the power and opportunity that I have as vice president to pick up the phone and call folks who take my call, to invite them to work with me and as a group on private investment, coupled with government investment and partnership with our African leaders in a way that we can actually move the needle in terms of economic development there. So, since the trip, which was $7 billion for the climate piece and $1 billion focused on women, we are growing the commitment and, in that way, exponentially growing the work, and I'm very excited about it. I've been convening these folks since our trip, since I last saw you, to keep it going, … to bring in additional partners, and to fortify the work. From a policy perspective, I feel very strongly that these partnerships are part of the roots that I'm intentionally planting so that this work has a lot of folks who are invested in it and will not just be the function of me being here. We will institutionalize it so that it can live and grow for generations to come. That's my intent.

NQQ: Your intention is being met with a lot of enthusiasm. Let's take a jaunt down memory lane with a few memorable photos. So, this was your arrival.

KH: Yes. Oh, my goodness.

NQQ: What was going through your mind moments after you stepped on African soil for the first time as VP?

Vice President Harris with Second Gentleman Dog Emhoff, Accra, March 2023

KH: I had a physical reaction and an emotional reaction. It was extraordinary. I felt an incredible sense of gratitude and joy. Oh, my goodness. It was incredible.

NQQ: And then there's this photo right here from Cape Coast Castle. What about this experience remains with you?

KH: Everything about that experience, which is about the pain, and if I may say just kind of … I don't know how you felt, but it was almost like a painful memory … when you just knew what happened in that place and the horrors of what happened. And the anger, especially being there at a time when extremist so-called leaders are pushing a narrative that would deny our children the ability to learn America's full history, including the part of the origin stories from that place.

Second Gentleman Doug Emhoff, Vice President Harris, and guide in the
dungeon of Cape Coast Castle, Ghana, March 2023

NQQ: (showing a picture of the vice president with Tanzanian president Samia Suluhu Hassan) Two historic firsts on the continent sharing the same stage. When she turned to you and referred to you as "my dear sister," what did that mean to you?

KH: Yes. That was familiar to me, I have to say. It was, I guess, in a way, that is also a first, that the vice president of the United States would feel a familiarity.

NQQ: Another first. What would your grandfather say about how you've been showing up as a world leader?

KH: He would be so proud. My grandfather cared so deeply about the future, and he cared deeply about the continent of Africa, beginning with Zambia. So, he—I think—he'd be very proud.

Vice President Harris with President Samia Suluhu Hassan, Tanzania, March 2023

NQQ: Madam Vice President, how do you want historians to remember your maiden voyage to the Motherland?

KH: It was the impetus of a new narrative on the relationship between the United States and the continent of Africa.

NQQ: And Madam Vice President, the last question is foodie to foodie. Inquiring minds want to know if you were building a menu for a West African themed dinner, would you put Ghanaian, Nigerian, or Senegalese jollof rice on the menu, and what protein would you pair it with?

KH: (laughing) Nope. No. I'm not doing that. I know better. I know the continent, and I am not answering that. But all of them are delicious.

NQQ: I'm half Ghanaian, so I'm biased.

Welcome Sign, Zambia, March 2023

Vice President Harris at Panuka Farms, Zambia, March 2023

KH: I know you are. I am not saying a thing. Let me just say that I am the first vice president—and I am certain of this—that travels the world and makes sure I go to the markets. Not the supermarket. I go to the market market to get whatever spices I can legally bring back. I am serious about that. I do not play around. I only eat local food when I am abroad, and I always go down and get to know the [hotel] chefs. Depending on what I have, I'll ask them for the recipe. I have some recipes. I actually have a really good jollof rice recipe, but I'm not telling you where I got it.

NQQ: Well, might I have an opportunity to sample it, maybe? (laughing, not laughing)

KH: Because I also have Nigerians in my family, so I gotta be careful about that. (laughing)

NQQ: Madam Vice President, thank you so much. There are a lot of people out there who said that following the Africa trip, they felt like you took it to the next level, showing up differently. You came back more dynamic than ever. Did you feel that?

KH: I am certain that I'm moving the needle on it, that I am certain both in terms of how I show up but also the work that I do internally to grow how we—out of this place— think about that place.

NQQ: Thank you so much.

Vice President Harris and Dr. Nii-Quartelai Quartey
in the White House, May 20, 2024

BEFORE EXITING VICE PRESIDENT'S WEST WING OFFICE

NQQ: I'm excited to share this journey with the public. You know, I never planned to write this book. I just thought "Okay. I'll go there and report about it on the news and/or produce a limited series podcast." What your team curated at your direction was so compelling; I absolutely had to write about it.

KH: Let me say something. I was very clear that we were not going there to talk about malaria, to talk about hungry babies. These are important issues—no question. That's not my point. My point is ... I mean, we didn't even get into the discussion just now about arts and culture, Afrobeats, how it is impacting—

NQQ: It's in the book.

KH: Good. I mean, there is so much there, and maybe it takes also someone who ... we know, there's more than just what we're fed. And so, when you know it, you know how to ask the questions to make sure that it's not going to be this cookie cutter kind of trip.

NQQ: Especially those of us that are a bridge between cultures. I mean, my dad's from Ghana, my mom's from Florida. They met at an HBCU in Texas and had me many years later in California. You know, so my story isn't all that different from your story.

KH: That's right. I'm very excited about our work there. That's why we were meeting with young tech entrepreneurs, the women that we met, farmers who were running ... the farming business. Yeah. Right.

NQQ: Powered by AI. Who would have ever thought on the continent that would be happening? It's in the book, too.

KH: We knew, and now everybody else will know. I'm glad you're writing this book.

Concluding Reflections

I see this book as a reflection and reexamination of US Vice President Kamala Harris, the continent of Africa, and ourselves. This is not just about Mildred in South Carolina, my mother in the Bay Area, or Uncle Eddie in Chicago. It is also about somebody's mother, auntie, uncle, or cousin in Accra,

Darsalam, and Lusaka. Our fates are intertwined, a concept that conservatives understand very well. That's why they are so busy on the continent pushing policies drenched in the anti-Black, anti-woman, and anti-LGBTQ values of the evangelical Right. The decisions we make around America's leadership will have direct consequences on the future of democracy and the quality of life available to all of us.

In the spirit of community and humility, I proudly share my informed perspective in hopes of inspiring more robust conversations, more thorough analyses, and higher levels of consciousness in a time such as this. There are people who may find things in this book uncomfortable or who may have differences of opinion, and they are entitled to that. If Project 2025—the Right-wing agenda that would roll back policies that have aided Black economic and social gains— is any indication, Black voters and voters of conscience everywhere cannot afford to sit out a single election. This is the time for more, not less, civic engagement. This does not mean we don't have critiques of the vice president and the current administration or the previous administration. It means the difference between holding someone accountable from across the table or over the fence and across the street. I hope the insights shared from this trip help to fill some of the gaps in the narrative around Vice President Harris, not only for Black voters, but all voters of conscience in the United States and beyond.

Let's not squander the opportunity to build a more perfect union at home and resist the division-inducing cultural tribalism that gives way to selective outrage. Let's feed the promise of counsel instead of cancel culture and become a more powerful demonstration of what's possible in a troubling and complicated world. We have a responsibility to ourselves, our ancestors and, people of African descent across the diaspora to do what we can, from where we are, with what we have.

ABOUT THE AUTHOR

Dr. Nii-Quartelai Quartey is a political journalist, Pepperdine University professor and prominent convener in the fields of dialogue and social change. Born into a Ghanaian-American family, Dr. Quartey holds a doctoral degree in organizational leadership and a master's degree in social entrepreneurship and change from Pepperdine University. He also holds a bachelor's degree in political science with a minor in critical approaches to leadership from University of Southern California. Throughout his career, he has been featured on various media outlets, including *The Oprah Winfrey Show*, CBS News, MSNBC, CNN, NewsNation, SiriusXM, TheGrio and as a daily news anchor for FOX Television and FOX SOUL. He currently serves as host of *A More Perfect Union* radio talk show and podcast produced by KBLA Talk 1580, the only Black-owned and operated talk station west of the Mississippi.

Before returning to his passion for political journalism, for over a decade Dr. Quartey had been actively engaged in policy advocacy efforts on issues ranging from civil and human rights to childhood obesity to senior issues. These experiences have been foundational to Dr. Quartey's distinctive approach to political journalism where he aspires to humanize leaders, listens for teachable moments, cautionary tales, and challenges underlying assumptions.

NOTES

CHAPTER 1

1. "Remarks by Vice President Harris to Ghanaian Youth at Black Star Gate." The White House website, March 28, 2023, accessed April 21, 2024, https://www.whitehouse.gov/briefing-room/speeches-remarks/2023/03/28/remarks-by-vice-president-harris-to-ghanaian-youth-at-black-star-gate/.
2. Ibid.
3. "Favorability of Vice President Kamala Harris in the United States as of March 2024." Statista website, accessed April 21, 2024, https://www.statista.com/statistics/1172346/share-us-adults-favorable-opinion-kamala-harris/.
4. Matt Stiles, Ryan Murphy, and Vanessa Martinez. "What does American think of Kamala Harris?" *Los Angeles Times* website, April 16, 2024, accessed February 29, 2024, https://www.latimes.com/projects/kamala-harris-approval-rating-polls-vs-biden-other-vps/.
5. Rashad Robinson, interview with author, March 7, 2024.
6. Ibid.

7. Ibid.

8. Ibid.

9. Terrance Woodbury, interview with author, February 9, 2024.

10. Eugene Daniels, interview with author, April 2, 2024.

11. Ibid.

12. "Remarks by Vice President Harris to Ghanaian Youth at Black Star Gate."

CHAPTER 2

1. "Colonial Ghana and the struggle for independence." Change for Ghana website, September 25, 2019, accessed April 21, https://www.changeforghana.org/post/colonial-ghana-and-the-struggle-for-independence.

2. Orla Ryan. "Ghana, 'booms' behind it, seeks more prosperity." Reuters website, August 9, 2007, accessed April 21, 2024, https://www.reuters.com/article/us-ghana-independence-celebration-idUSL0146677420070306/.

3. "From Kwame Nkrumah." The Martin Luther King, Jr. Research and Education Institute, Stanford University website, accessed April 21, 2024, https://kinginstitute.stanford.edu/king-papers/documents/kwame-nkrumah.

4. Wendi Maloney. "African-American History Month: First Pan-African Congress." Library of Congress Blogs, February 19, 2019, accessed April 21, 2024, https://blogs.loc.gov/loc/2019/02/african-american-history-month-first-pan-african-congress/.

5. Derrick Johnson, interview with author, February 23, 2024.

6. Ibid.
7. Ibid.
8. Ibid.
9. "Remarks by Vice President Harris at a State Banquet Hosted by President Akufo-Addo of Ghana." The White House website, March 27, 2023, accessed April 21, 2024, https://www.whitehouse.gov/briefing-room/speeches-remarks/2023/03/27/remarks-by-vice-president-harris-at-a-state-banquet-hosted-by-president-akufo-addo-of-ghana/.
10. Ibid.
11. Ibid.
12. Ibid.
13. Jessica Ankomah. "How Ghana's 'Year of Return' Sparked a Pan-African Phenomenon." Culture Trip website, April 17, 2020, accessed April 21, 2024, https://theculturetrip.com/africa/ghana/articles/how-ghanas-year-of-return-sparked-a-pan-african-phenomenon#:~:text=Ghana%E2%80%99s%20Year%20of%20Return%20is%20one%20of%20the,was%20President%20Akufo-Addo%E2%80%99s%20call%20to%20return%20so%20poignant%3F.
14. Derrick Johnson interview.
15. "Share of travel and tourism in Africa's Gross Domestic Product (GDP) from 2019 to 2023." Statista website, accessed April 21, 2024, https://www.statista.com/statistics/1320400/share-of-travel-and-tourism-in-africas-gross-domestic-product/.
16. Davidmac O. Ekeocha, Jonathan E. Ogbuabor, Anthony Orji, Ugbor I. Kalu. "International tourism and economic growth

in Africa: A post-global financial crisis analysis." *Tourism Management Perspectives* 40, (October 2021), https://doi.org/10.1016/j.tmp.2021.100896.

17. Anonymous US-African affairs expert, interview with author, January 30, 2024.

18. Ibid.

19. "Beyond the Return: A Decade of African Renaissance." Beyond the Return website, accessed April 21, 2024, https://beyondthereturngh.com/.

20. "About 'Beyond the Return.'" Visit Ghana website, accessed April 21, 2024, https://visitghana.com/beyond-the-return

21. "Beyond the Return."

22. "About 'Beyond the Return.'"

23. David Maimela. "Pan-Africanism of the 21st Century – Challenges and Prospects." *The Journal of the Helen Suzman Foundation* 71, (November 2013): 34–39, https://hsf.org.za/publications/focus/copy_of_focus-71-state-nation/pan-africanism-of-21st-century-d-maimela.pdf

CHAPTER 3

1. Emmanuel Akinwotu. "Ghanaian LGBTQ+ centre closes after threats and abuse." *The Guardian* website, February 25, 2021, accessed April 21, 2024, https://www.theguardian.com/global-development/2021/feb/25/lgbtq-ghanaians-under-threat-after-backlash-against-new-support-centre.

2. "Remarks by Vice President Harris and President Akufo-Addo of the Republic of Ghana in Joint Press Conference." The White House website, March 27, 2023, accessed April 21, 2024, https://www.whitehouse.gov/briefing-room/

speeches-remarks/2023/03/27/remarks-by-vice-president-harris-and-president-akufo-addo-of-the-republic-of-ghana-in-joint-press-conference/.

3. "FACT SHEET: President Biden and G7 Leaders Launch Build Back Better World (B3W) Partnership." The White House website, June 12, 2021, accessed April 21, 2024, https://www.whitehouse.gov/briefing-room/statements-releases/2021/06/12/fact-sheet-president-biden-and-g7-leaders-launch-build-back-better-world-b3w-partnership/.

4. "Remarks by Vice President Harris and President Akufo-Addo of the Republic of Ghana in Joint Press Conference."

5. Thomas Naadi. "Ghana passes bill making identifying as LGBTQ+ illegal." *BBC News* website, February 28, 2024, accessed April 21, 2024, https://www.bbc.com/news/world-africa-68353437.

6. Thomas Naadi. "Ghana's anti-LGBTQ+ bill: President Akufo-Addo to wait for Supreme Court ruling." *BBC News* website, March 5, 2024, accessed April 21, 2024, https://www.bbc.com/news/world-africa-68477878.

7. Rashad Robinson, interview with author, March 7, 2024.

8. "Ghana GDP." Trading Economics website, accessed April 21, 2024, https://tradingeconomics.com/ghana/gdp#:~:text=The%20Gross%20Domestic%20Product%20%28GDP%29%20in%20Ghana%20was,Ghana%20represents%200.03%20percent%20of%20the%20world%20economy.

9. Rashad Robinson interview.

10. Khatondi Soita Wepukhulu. "Top Ghanaian doctors use misinformation to train nurses in 'conversion therapy.'" openDemocracy website, July 28, 2022, accessed

April 21, 2024, https://www.opendemocracy.net/en/5050/ ghana-anti-lgbtiq-bill-conversion-therapy-training-doctors/.

11. "Uganda passes a law making it a crime to identify as LGBTQ." *Reuters* website, March 21, 2023, accessed April 21, 2024, https://www.reuters.com/world/africa/ uganda-passes-bill-banning-identifying-lgbtq-2023-03-21/.

12. Emmanuel Akinwotu. "Blackmail, prejudice and persecution: gay rights in Nigeria." *The Guardian* website, March 30, 2018, accessed April 21, 2024, https://www. theguardian.com/global-development/2018/mar/30/ blackmail-prejudice-persecution-gay-rights-nigeria.

13. Ardo Hazzad. "Nigerian Islamic court orders death by stoning for men convicted of homosexuality." *Reuters* website, July 2, 2022, accessed April 21, 2024, https://www. reuters.com/world/africa/nigerian-islamic-court-orders-death-by-stoning-men-convicted-homosexuality-2022-07-02/.

14. Mariel Ferragamo and Kali Robinson. "Where African countries stand in their struggle toward more inclusive LGBTQ+ laws." PBS website, June 18, 2023, accessed April 21, 2024, https://www.pbs.org/newshour/world/ where-african-countries-stand-in-their-struggle-toward-more-inclusive-lgbtq-laws.

15. Aaron Rakhetsi. "6 Countries in Africa That Have Legalized Same-Sex Relationships in the Past 10 Years." Global Citizen website, February 25, 2021, accessed April 21, 2024, https://www.globalcitizen.org/en/content/ countries-legalized-same-sex-relationships-africa/.

16. Laura Begley Bloom. "Travel Safety Report: 20 Worst Places For Gay Travelers In 2021." *Forbes* website, March 23, 2021,

accessed April 21, 2024, https://www.forbes.com/sites/
laurabegleybloom/2021/03/23/crime-report-20-riskiest-
places-for-gay-travelers-and-the-5-safest/?sh=5081af9d6d1b.

CHAPTER 4

1. "Remarks by Vice President Harris During Visit to Vibrate
    Studio." The White House website, March 27, 2023, accessed
    April 21, 2024, https://www.whitehouse.gov/briefing-room/
    speeches-remarks/2023/03/27/remarks-by-vice-president-
    harris-during-visit-to-vibrate-studio/.

2. "Arts and Cultural Production Satellite Account, U.S.
    and Stages, 2020." Bureau of Economic Analysis website,
    March 15, 2022, accessed April 21, 2024, https://www.
    bea.gov/news/2022/arts-and-cultural-production-satellite-
    account-us-and-states-2020.

3. Ojoma Ochai. "Africa's creative industries on the
    move, breaking barriers." Africa Renewal website,
    December 7, 2021, accessed April 21, 2024, https://
    www.un.org/africarenewal/magazine/december-2021/
    africas-creative-industries-move-breaking-barriers.

4. "Landmark report highlights untapped potential of
    Africa's film industry." United Nations website, October
    5, 2021, accessed April 21, 2024, https://news.un.org/en/
    story/2021/10/1102232.

5. "UNESCO spotlights growth potential of Africa's film
    industry." UNESCO website, April 12, 2022, accessed
    April 21, 2024, https://www.unesco.org/en/articles/
    unesco-spotlights-growth-potential-africas-film-industry.

6. "How Much is Digital Video Piracy Costing the U.S. Economy?" NCTA website, July 2, 2019, accessed April 21, 2024, https://www.ncta.com/whats-new/how-much-is-digital-video-piracy-costing-the-us-economy#:~:text=A%20new%20study%20estimates%20that%20the%20U.S.%20economy,year%20as%20a%20result%20of%20global%20digital%20piracy.

7. "Nigeria enacts new Copyright Act." Adams & Adams website, March 30, 2023, accessed April 21, 2024, https://www.adams.africa/africa-general/nigeria-enacts-new-copyright-act/.

8. "FAQs About The South African Film Industry." National Film and Video Foundation website, accessed April 21, 2024, https://www.nfvf.co.za/faqs-about-the-south-african-film-industry/

9. Andrew England. "Booming film industry boosts South Africa's economy." *Financial Times* website, September 5, 2014, accessed April 21, 2024, https://www.ft.com/content/6cce315e-3420-11e4-b81c-00144feabdc0.

10. Amanda Visser. "Massive untapped potential for SA film industry." Moneyweb website, October 20, 2021, accessed April 21, 2024, https://www.moneyweb.co.za/news/south-africa/massive-untapped-potential-for-sa-film-industry/.

11. "Remarks by Vice President Harris at a Celebration for the 50th Anniversary of Hip-Hop." The White House website, September 9, 2023, accessed April 21, 2024, https://www.whitehouse.gov/briefing-room/speeches-remarks/2023/09/09/remarks-by-vice-president-harris-at-a-celebration-for-the-50th-anniversary-of-hip-hop/.

CHAPTER 5

1. "Cape Coast Castle, Cape Coast (1653)." Ghana Museums and Monuments Board website, accessed April 21, 2024, https://gmmb.gov.gh/cape-coast-castle-cape-coast-1653/.

2. Richard Cavendish. "Elmina Castle." Britannica website, accessed April 21, 2024, https://www.britannica.com/place/Elmina-Castle.

3. "Cape Coast Castle, Cape Coast (1653)."

4. "Cape Coast Castle." The Colonial Williamsburg Foundation website, accessed April 21, 2024, https://slaveryandremembrance.org/articles/article/?id=A0103.

5. "The triangular trade: Slave factories on the African coast." *BBC* website, accessed April 21, 2024, https://www.bbc.co.uk/bitesize/guides/zqv7hyc/revision/7.

6. "Remarks by Vice President Harris at Cape Coast Castle." The White House website, March 28, 2023, accessed April 21, 2024, https://www.whitehouse.gov/briefing-room/speeches-remarks/2023/03/28/remarks-by-vice-president-harris-at-cape-coast-castle/.

7. Kenneth Walden (@2rawtooreal), "VP Kamala Harris Hair Update!!! So her silk press lost the battle when she made it to Cape Coast castle a black womans hair ain't safe in humidity. That heat was waiting for her at the door", X, March 28, 2023, 10:19 a.m., https://twitter.com/2RawTooReal/status/1640765460038778892.

8. Eugene Scott. "Why some African Americans are questioning Kamala Harris's blackness." *The Washington Post* website, June 28, 2019, accessed April 21, 2024,

https://www.washingtonpost.com/politics/2019/02/14/why-some-african-americans-are-questioning-kamala-harriss-blackness/.

9. Robin Givehan. "Kamala Harris grew up in a mostly White world. Then she went to a Black university in a Black city." *The Washington Post* website, January 11, 2021, accessed April 21, 2024, https://www.washingtonpost.com/lifestyle/2021/01/11/kamala-harris-howard-university-black-city/.

10. Charlamagne tha God, DJ Envy, and Kamala Harris. "Kamala Harris Talks 2020 Presidential Run, Legalizing Marijuana, Criminal Justice Reform + More." The Breakfast Club Studio, streamed live on February 11, 2019, YouTube video, 44:18, https://www.youtube.com/watch?v=Kh_wQUjeaTk&t=3s.

11. Charles Blow. "Kamala Harris isn't Americans' 'Momala.' She's our vice president." Editorial, *The New York Times* website, May 1, 2024, accessed May 27, 2024, https://www.nytimes.com/2024/05/01/opinion/drew-barrymore-kamala-harris.html.

12. Kim Parker and Amanda Barroso. "In Vice President Kamala Harris, we can see how American has changed." Pew Research Center website, February 25, 2021, accessed April 21, 2024, https://www.pewresearch.org/short-reads/2021/02/25/in-vice-president-kamala-harris-we-can-see-how-america-has-changed/.

13. Terrance Woodbury, interview with author, February 9, 2024.

14. Ibid.

CHAPTER 6

1. "Remarks by Vice President Harris and President Samia Suluhu Hassan of Tanzania in Joint Press Statements." The White House website, March 30, 2023, accessed April 21, 2024, https://www.whitehouse.gov/briefing-room/speeches-remarks/2023/03/30/remarks-by-vice-president-harris-and-president-samia-suluhu-Hassan-of-tanzania-in-joint-press-statements/.
2. Ibid.
3. Ibid.
4. Jason Burke. "Tanzanian government cracks down on opposition after disputed election." *The Guardian* website, November 2, 2020, accessed April 21, 2024, https://www.theguardian.com/world/2020/nov/02/tanzanian-opposition-figures-arrested-after-disputed-election.
5. "Remarks by Vice President Harris and President Samia Suluhu Hassan of Tanzania in Joint Press Statements."
6. Ibid.
7. Charles Stith, interview with author, January 10, 2024.
8. Ibid.

CHAPTER 7

1. "Remarks by Vice President Harris in Meeting with Private Sector and Philanthropic Leaders on Digital Inclusion in Africa." The White House website, April 1, 2023, accessed April 21, 2024, https://www.whitehouse.gov/briefing-room/speeches-remarks/2023/04/01/remarks-by-vice-president-

harris-in-meeting-with-private-sector-and-philanthropic-leaders-on-digital-inclusion-in-africa/.

2. Ibid.

3. Ibid.

4. "Policy Brief: Digital inclusion in the Women, Peace and Security Agenda in Africa." United Nations website, July 11, 2022, accessed April 21, 2024, https://www.un.org/shestandsforpeace/sites/www.un.org.shestandsforpeace/files/unoau_policy_brief_v3_0.pdf.

5. "Fact Sheet: Vice President Harris Launches Global Initiatives on the Economic Empowerment of Women, Totaling over $1 Billion." The White House website, March 29, 2023, https://www.whitehouse.gov/briefing-room/statements-releases/2023/03/29/fact-sheet-vice-president-harris-launches-global-initiatives-on-the-economic-empowerment-of-women-totaling-over-1-billion/.

6. Ibid.

7. Ibid.

8. Ibid.

9. Marguerite Reardon. "The digital divide has left millions of school kids behind." CNET website, May 5, 2021, accessed April 21, 2024, https://www.cnet.com/home/internet/the-digital-divide-has-left-millions-of-school-kids-behind/.

10. "Startling digital divides in distance learning emerge." UNESCO website, April 21, 2020, accessed April 21, 2024, https://www.unesco.org/en/articles/startling-digital-divides-distance-learning-emerge.

11. Marguerite Reardon. "The digital divide has left millions of school kids behind."

12. "Remarks by Vice President Harris in Meeting with Private Sector and Philanthropic Leaders on Digital Inclusion in Africa."
13. Rashad Robinson, interview with author, March 7, 2024.
14. Christin Roby. "Rwanda's "solar smart kiosk" provides digital solutions to rural mobile phone users." Devex website, April 3, 2017, accessed April 21, 2024, https://www.devex.com/news/rwanda-s-solar-smart-kiosk-provides-digital-solutions-to-rural-mobile-phone-users-89956.

CHAPTER 8

1. "Remarks by Vice President Harris and President Hichilema of Zambia in Joint Press Conference." The White House website, March 31, 2023, accessed April 27, 2024, https://www.whitehouse.gov/briefing-room/speeches-remarks/2023/03/31/remarks-by-vice-president-harris-and-president-hichilema-of-zambia-in-joint-press-conference/
2. Ibid.
3. Ibid.
4. Ibid.
5. Ibid.
6. Derrick Johnson, interview with author, February 23, 2024.
7. Ibid.
8. Ibid.
9. Dr. Wayne A. I. Frederick, interview with author, February 27, 2024.
10. Ibid.
11. Ibid.

12. Charles Stith, interview with author, January 10, 2024.

13. Frik Els. "CHART: China's stranglehold on electric car battery supply chain." The Northern Miner Group website, April 16, 2020, accessed April 21, 2024, https://www.mining.com/chart-chinas-stranglehold-on-electric-car-battery-supply-chain/.

14. "Graphite." TanzaniaInvest website, accessed April 21, 2024, https://www.tanzaniainvest.com/graphite#:~:text=Tanzania%E2%80%99s%20largest%20graphite%20deposits%20are%20located%20in%20the,Jumbo.%20Production%20stages%20have%20not%20been%20reached%20yet.

15. "PEPFAR." HIV.gov website, accessed April 21, 2024, https://www.hiv.gov/federal-response/pepfar-global-aids/pepfar#:~:text=The%20U.S.%20President%27s%20Emergency%20Plan%20for%20AIDS%20Relief,in%20more%20than%2050%20countries%20around%20the%20world.

16. Charles Stith interview.

17. "The Millennium Challenge Account." The White House – President George W. Bush website, accessed April 21, 2024, https://georgewbush-whitehouse.archives.gov/infocus/developingnations/millennium.html.

18. Charles Stith interview.

19. "Africa." Millennium Challenge Corporation website, accessed April 21, 2024, https://www.mcc.gov/where-we-work/region/africa/#:~:text=benefited%20an%20estimated%2094%20million%20Africans%2C%20improved%20the,have%20legal%20rights%20and%20protections%20over%20their%20land.

20. Errin Haines, interview with author, April 2, 2024.

21. Ibid.

22. Ibid.

23. Ibid.

24. "Castro, Bass, Chu, Haaland, Titus Introduce New Legislation to Promot State Department Diversity and Inclusion." Joaquin Castro website, December 9. 2020, accessed May 3, 2024, https://castro.house.gov/media-center/press-releases/castro-bass-chu-haaland-titus-introduce-new-legislation-to-promote-state-department-diversity-and-inclusion

CHAPTER 9

1. "Remarks by Vice President Harris on Increasing Climate Resilience, Adaptation, and Mitigation Across Africa." The White House website, April 1, 2023, accessed April 27, 2024, https://www.whitehouse.gov/briefing-room/speeches-remarks/2023/04/01/remarks-by-vice-president-harris-on-increasing-climate-resilience-adaptation-and-mitigation-across-africa/

2. Ibid.

3. Ibid.

4. Cathryn Birch, John Marsham, and Sarah Chapman. "Climate change will cause more African children to die from hot weather." DownToEarth website, August 24, 2022, accessed April 21, 2024, https://www.downtoearth.org.in/blog/africa/climate-change-will-cause-more-african-children-to-die-from-hot-weather-84514.

5. "Malaria." World Health Organization website, December 4, 2023, accessed April 21, 2024, https://www.who.int/news-room/fact-sheets/detail/malaria.

6. Hassan Sachedina, Marius van der Vyver, and Tim Tear. "Africa's remaining forests are under pressure: This is no time to sideline forest carbon markets." World Economic Forum website, September 23, 2021, accessed April 21, 2024, https://www.weforum.org/agenda/2021/09/africa-s-remaining-forests-and-wildlife-are-under-increasing-pressure-this-is-no-time-to-sideline-forest-carbon-markets/.

7. "Remarks by Vice President Harris on Increasing Climate Resilience, Adaptation, and Mitigation Across Africa."

8. Jason B. Johnson. "SAN FRANCISCO / D.A. creates environmental unit / 3 staff team takes on crime mostly affecting the poor." SFGATE website, June 1, 2005, accessed April 21, 2024, https://www.sfgate.com/crime/article/SAN-FRANCISCO-D-A-creates-environmental-unit-2666667.php.

9. "National Environmental Scorecard: Senator Kamala Harris (D)." LCV website, accessed April 21, 2024, https://scorecard.lcv.org/moc/kamala-harris.

10. Laura Paddison and Annette Choi. "As climate chaos accelerates, which countries are polluting the most?" CNN website, January 2, 2024, accessed April 21, 2024, https://www.cnn.com/interactive/2023/12/us/countries-climate-change-emissions-cop28/.

CHAPTER 11

1. Sarah Carter. "Ghana's parliament passes strict new anti-LGBTQ legislation to extend sentences and expand scope." CBS News website, February 28, 2024, accessed

April 28, 2024, https://www.cbsnews.com/news/ghana-anti-lgbtq-legislation-passed-by-parliament/.

2. Ibid.

3. Isabela Espadas Barros Leal. "Schools are increasingly locations for hate crimes, FBI data shows." *NBC News* website, January 30, 2024, accessed April 27, 2024, https://www.nbcnews.com/nbc-out/out-news/schools-are-increasingly-location-hate-crimes-fbi-data-shows-rcna136341

4. Taylor Telford. "They invest in Black women. A lawsuit claims it's discrimination." *The Washington Post* website, August 25, 2023, accessed April 21, 2024, https://www.washingtonpost.com/business/2023/08/26/dei-lawsuit-black-businesses-fearless-fund-edward-blum/.

5. Anthony Robledo. "Complaint accuses George Floyd scholarship of discriminating against non-Black students." *USA Today* website, March 29, 2024, accessed April 21, 2024, https://www.usatoday.com/story/news/nation/2024/03/28/george-floyd-university-scholarship-sued-discrimination/73138297007/.

6. Dr. Wayne A. I. Frederick, interview with author, February 27, 2024.

7. Josh Boak and Seung Min Kim. "Special counsel alleged Biden couldn't recall personal milestones. His response: 'My memory is fine.'" *AP News* website, February 8, 2024, accessed April 21, 2024, https://apnews.com/article/biden-memory-age-special-counsel-report-doj-f4232bc8316e556ed467185b67c3e0a8.

8. Samantha Latson. "'Gratuitous': Harris slams Hur report, defends Biden." *Politico* website, February 9, 2024, accessed April 21, 2024, https://www.politico.com/news/2024/02/09/biden-hur-special-counsel-harris-00140744.

9. Ibid.